HERBERT FERBER
SCULPTURE, PAINTING, DRAWING: 1945-1980

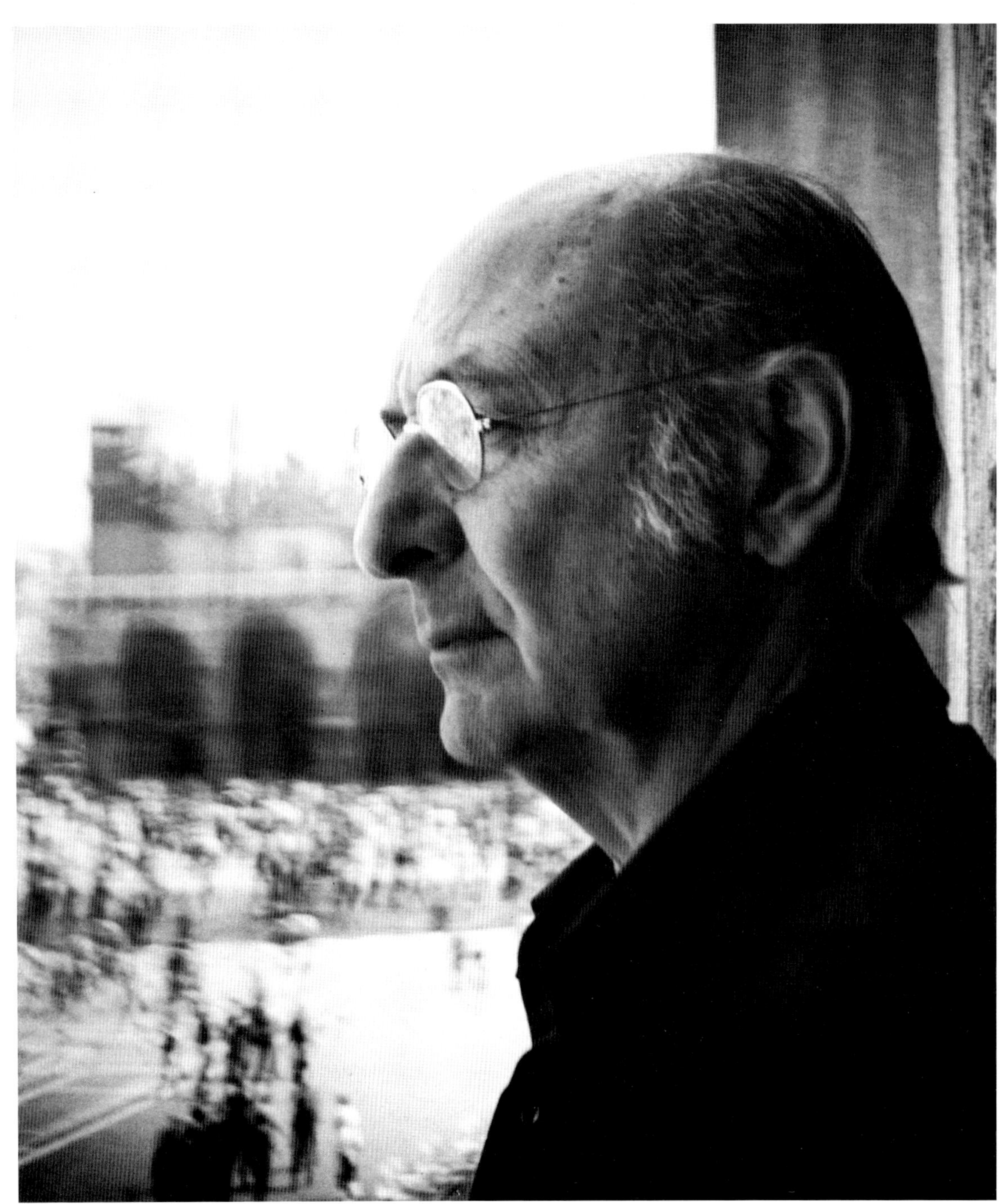

Herbert Ferber
Sculpture, Painting, Drawing: 1945-1980

William C. Agee

Chronology by Phyllis Tuchman

The Museum of Fine Arts, Houston 1983

Funding for the catalogue was provided by the McAshan Educational and Charitable Trust, Houston and by Mr. George S. Heyer, Jr.

Exhibition dates:
The Museum of Fine Arts, Houston
May 1-June 28, 1981

The Des Moines Art Center
November 23, 1981-January 3, 1982

Cover: *Notch View,* 1978. Steel. 76 x 144 x 76 in. (193.1 x 365.7 x 193.1 cm.)
Diane and Steve Jacobson, East Hampton, New York

Frontispiece: Ferber at the Piazza San Marco, Venice, 1973.

Designed by Layne and Bales
Typeset by Wordseller, Houston
Printed and bound by Fidelity Printing Company, Houston

Printed in the United States of America

Library of Congress Catalog Card Number 80-85455

ISBN 0-89090-005-1

The Museum of Fine Arts, Houston, 1001 Bissonnet, Houston, Texas 77005

Contents

Lenders to the Exhibition

Abrams Family Collection, New York

Stephen B. Chase, Rancho Mirage, California

Congregation Beth Israel, Houston

Edith Ferber, New York

Herbert Ferber, Courtesy of M. Knoedler & Co., Inc., New York

Henry V. Heuser, Jr., Louisville, Kentucky

Diane and Steve Jacobson, East Hampton, New York

Murray Financial Corporation, Dallas

Mr. and Mrs. Fulton Murray, Dallas

Sharon and Neil Norry, Rochester, New York

Mr. and Mrs. Robert Pergament, Kings Point, New York

Mr. and Mrs. Robert Postal, Great Neck, New York

The Prudential Insurance Company of America, Newark, New Jersey

Richard L. Rubin, Bedford, New York

Private collectors

Albright-Knox Art Gallery, Buffalo, New York

The Metropolitan Museum of Art, New York

The Museum of Fine Arts, Houston

The Museum of Modern Art, New York

National Gallery of Art, Washington, D.C.

Georges Pompidou Art & Culture Foundation, New York

Rutgers University Art Gallery, New Brunswick, New Jersey

Storm King Art Center, Mountainville, New York

Whitney Museum of American Art, New York

Foreword

On April 30, 1981, the day his retrospective exhibition opened at The Museum of Fine Arts, Houston for its members and guests, Herbert Ferber celebrated his seventy-fifth birthday. He had been a serious artist for fifty years, an important artist for thirty-five years. It would be difficult to document fully a career of that length, no matter how large the exhibition, and the some sixty sculptures, twenty paintings, and fifty drawings included only could summarize the evolution of his art since 1945. The difficulty was compounded because many of Ferber's most important works have been public architectural commissions which are installed permanently and could not be moved. These works are illustrated in this catalogue and were represented in the exhibition by large photomural blowups and, where possible, by small working models.

In order to illuminate most effectively Ferber's art within these limitations, some decisions as to the composition and focus of the exhibition had to be made. The exhibition began with the year 1945, when Ferber made the first works that announced his place in the emergence of the new American sculpture, although a few representative pieces from the years 1932-1945 are reproduced and discussed briefly. (A fuller discussion of Ferber's work from these years is given in E. C. Goossen's book on the artist which was published simultaneously with the opening of the exhibition.) Ferber's reputation was established first by his Surrealist work of 1945-1950. It was secured further by the more formal, calligraphic works of the fifties which culminated in the *Sculpture as Environment,* commissioned by the Whitney Museum of American Art in 1960 and shown there in 1961. Since then he has been known primarily for his *Homage to Piranesi* series — the cages — which he began in 1961 and which today still yields some of his best art.

What has not been recognized widely is the exhilarating way in which he has revitalized his work in the last fifteen years by means of a fresh formal syntax quite distinct from that of the cages. This work stands as a highly significant sculptural achievement, and in order to focus on these more recent developments, over half the sculptures in the exhibition dated from the mid-1960s to the present. Since this catalogue is being published after the opening of the exhibition, it is possible to discuss his most recent work and to include installation photographs.

Ferber came to art first through drawing and then through etching, and in the early thirties he was occupied as much with painting as with sculpture. Since then he has undertaken two serious and sustained painting campaigns, one dating from 1958 to 1963, the other from 1973 to the present, and since 1960 he has had frequent exhibitions of his paintings. This exhibition included paintings from both periods, but only a few are reproduced here, since their close color values often render black-and-white reproductions almost invisible.

Ferber is a compulsive draftsman, and drawing has been intrinsic to his working method both as a sculptor and, to a lesser extent, as a painter. The drawings are all complete works of art in themselves and consist of three types: (1) studies for existing works, some of which were included in the exhibition, others not, (2) studies for pieces not realized, but which give further insight into the range of his sculptural ideas, and (3) drawings which are more truly small paintings and which relate to both his painting and sculpture.

I urge the reader to consult the chronology by Phyllis Tuchman, since the essay here contains a minimum of biographical information; the writings of E. C. Goossen and Wayne Andersen should also be consulted for his biography. This essay tries not to repeat areas which they have covered well and which are noted in the text and footnotes. This enabled me to give more emphasis to the later work which the show itself emphasized and to explore ideas pertaining to the earlier work which have not received as much attention.

Acknowledgments

On behalf of the Boards of Trustees of The Museum of Fine Arts, Houston and the Des Moines Art Center, I extend my warmest appreciation to the many people who helped realize this exhibition and catalogue. First, I must thank the lenders whose generosity made the exhibition possible in the most fundamental sense. Sculpture always is difficult to pack and ship, but the lenders, whose names are listed separately, extended every courtesy to enable us to exhibit thirty-five years of the artist's work. I also wish to thank the institutions and private collectors who granted permission to reproduce works by the artist that were not in the show.

The exhibition coincided with the publication of *Herbert Ferber* by E. C. Goossen, with a chronology and bibliography by Phyllis Tuchman. Mr. Goossen has championed and written about Ferber's art for more than twenty-five years, and his study and counsel stand behind my own work. With Ms. Tuchman's kind permission, her excellent and thorough chronology is included here with only minor changes and additions. She generously also has provided other important information and documentation. To them both I extend my deepest gratitude. Robert Abrams and Phyllis Benjamin of The Abbeville Press, New York, publishers of Mr. Goossen's book, have my thanks for granting permission to include Ms. Tuchman's material. It is my hope that Mr. Goossen's book and this catalogue will be read together and that they will serve as complementary volumes.

I am indebted to Wayne V. Andersen, whose lectures and publications are basic to the understanding of American sculpture of the last fifty years. His book *American Sculpture in Process: 1930-1970* (Boston: New York Graphic Society, 1975) has clarified what was previously a dimly perceived history, and in 1962, while curator at the Walker Art Center, Mr. Andersen organized Ferber's first retrospective. His catalogue published on that occasion still is indispensable.

I first came to know Ferber's art in depth in 1968-1969 while I was associate curator at The Museum of Modern Art. At that time, William Rubin asked me to work with him on the exhibition *The New American Painting and Sculpture: The First Generation,* and I thus owe him a great debt. In planning and organizing the Ferber exhibition, I have received invaluable encouragement and perceptive observations which have guided me throughout. I am also grateful to him, as well as to John Elderfield, director of the Department of Drawings, at The Museum of Modern Art, for their willingness to honor all of my requests for loans from The Museum of Modern Art.

Many of the artist's papers, including important letters, transcripts, and other documents, have been donated to the Archives of American Art, an institution that is crucial to all scholars and students of American art. I wish to thank William E. Woolfenden, director; Garnett McCoy, senior archivist; Jemy Hammond of the New York office; and Sandra Curtis Levy and Terrell James of the Houston office for extending every courtesy in making this material available to me.

A special acknowledgment is due the staff of The Museum of Fine Arts, Houston, which ably has assisted me at every stage. Karen Bremer, assistant curator, has been instrumental in realizing the exhibition and catalogue from the project's inception. Her diligent research lies behind every aspect of the exhibition and catalogue, as does her painstaking work in preparing the checklist, and she has my deepest appreciation. Linda Nelson Shearouse, librarian, performed at her usual high standard in providing bibliographical sources and documentation, for which I owe her my warmest gratitude. Anne Feltus edited the catalogue with her customary skill and tenacity, and I am most appreciative of her willingness to assume this demanding task. I would also like to thank Ron Jarvis for his tireless efforts in seeing the catalogue through production at every step. Dorwayne Clements typed and retyped the manuscript not only with the greatest skill, but with unstinting patience. Donna Fleming, Lainie Gordon, Charlotte Callager, Gail Petty, and Jane Rogers also provided their special skills, as did Erik Binas, Debby Satten, and Laura Russell of the Preparations Department. Edward Mayo, registrar, and his staff, Marilyn Outlaw Allen, Charles Carroll, and Maggie Olvey, all extended their help with the logistics of assembling the exhibition.

We have been fortunate to have the unstinting support of the artist's present gallery, M. Knoedler and Co., Inc., as well as his former dealer, André Emmerich. To Lawrence Rubin, president of M. Knoedler and Co., Inc., and to Anne Freedman, director of contemporary art at the gallery, as well as the registrar, Marian Ruggles, I extend my warmest appreciation for their kind and vital assistance with every aspect of this project. André Emmerich kindly provided every courtesy, as did his former associate Robert Miller, who has since established his own gallery in New York.

Laura Westby, the artist's assistant, deserves a special note of thanks from everyone concerned with the exhibition. She was tireless in overseeing the preparation, packing, shipping, and documentation of Ferber's work, and I owe her my deepest appreciation.

The Des Moines Art Center long has recognized Ferber's importance. His 1962 retrospective traveled to Des Moines, and director James Demetrion was instrumental in securing the commission of a major work for the City of Ottumwa, Iowa, in 1977. It is always a pleasure to work with Mr. Demetrion, and I am delighted that he enthusiastically joined in sharing this exhibition. I am deeply grateful to him and his able staff, especially Peggy Patrick, for its assistance and support.

I would like to extend my special thanks to the McAshan Educational and Charitable Trust for its enthusiastic response to Ferber's art. A generous grant from the Trust in support in the early stages of the catalogue was crucial. Thereafter, a gift from Mr. George S. Heyer, Jr. made the completion of this catalogue possible, and he has my deepest and most enduring gratitude.

Finally I must extend my special gratitude to Herbert Ferber and his wife Edith. They have done everything, and more, that I have asked in the long and, I know, often tedious process of assembling the exhibition and catalogue with a grace and kindness that went beyond any normal responsibility. It has been a rare privilege to work with them, and in turn I only can hope that I have done some justice to the artist's achievement.

W.C.A.

List of Color Plates

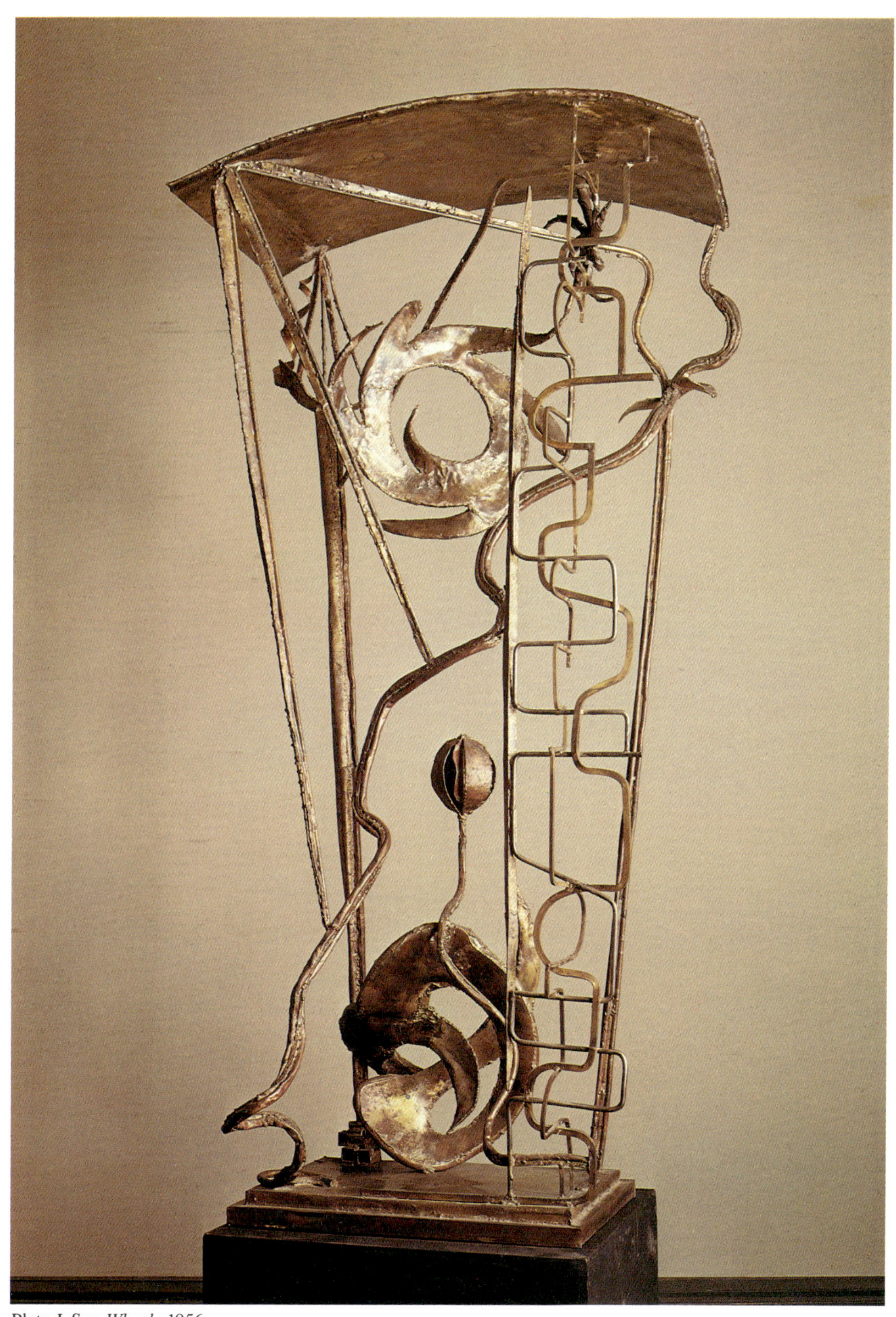

Plate I *Sun Wheel.* 1956.
Brass, copper, and stainless steel. $56\frac{1}{4}$ x 29 x 19 in. (142.9 x 73.7 x 48.3 cm.)
Collection Whitney Museum of American Art, New York. 56.18

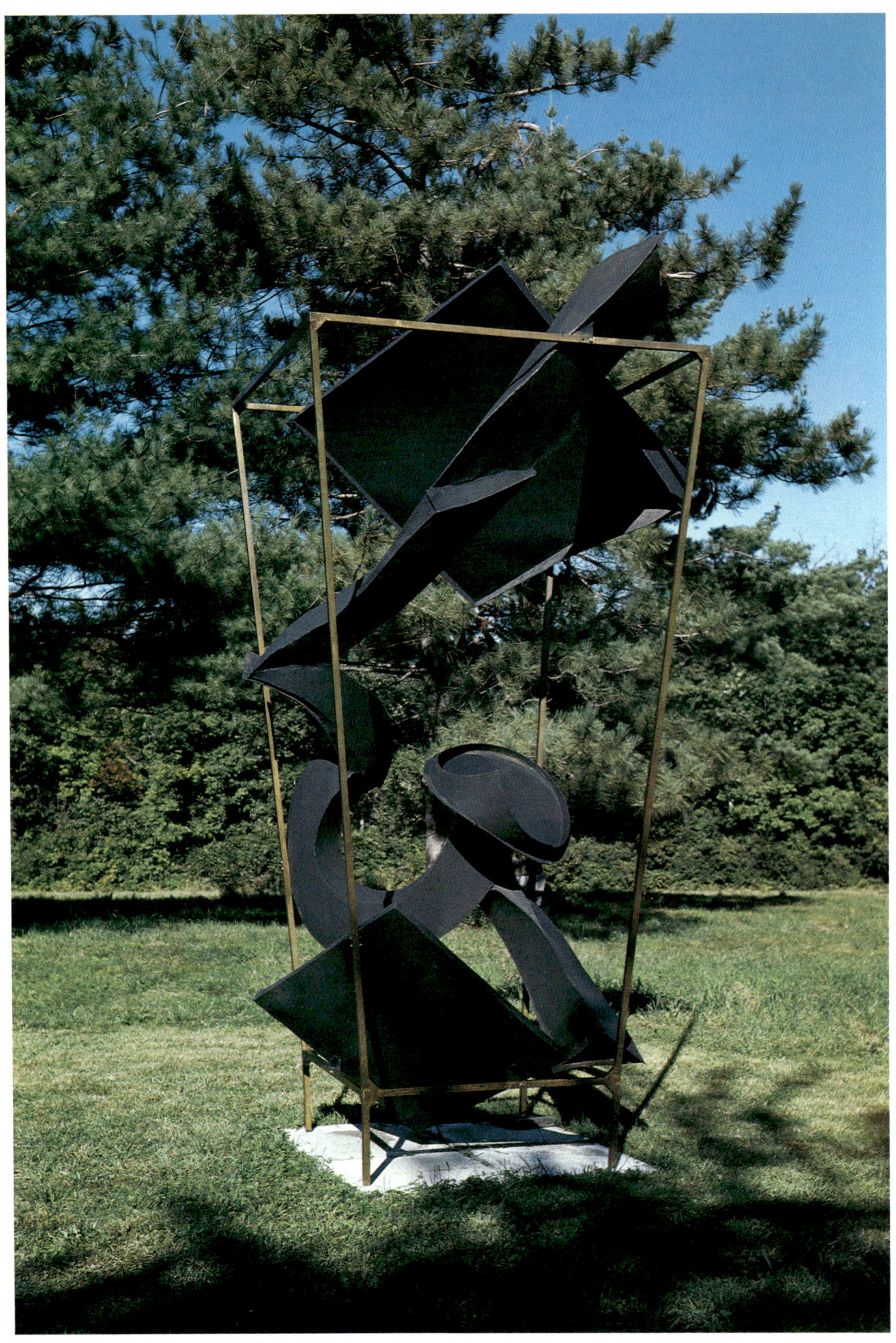

Plate II *Two Squares with Disk II*, 1970.
Cor-Ten steel and brass. 138 x 72 x 72 in. (350.5 x 182.9 x 182.9 cm.)
Collection Herbert Ferber,
Courtesy of M. Knoedler & Co., Inc., New York

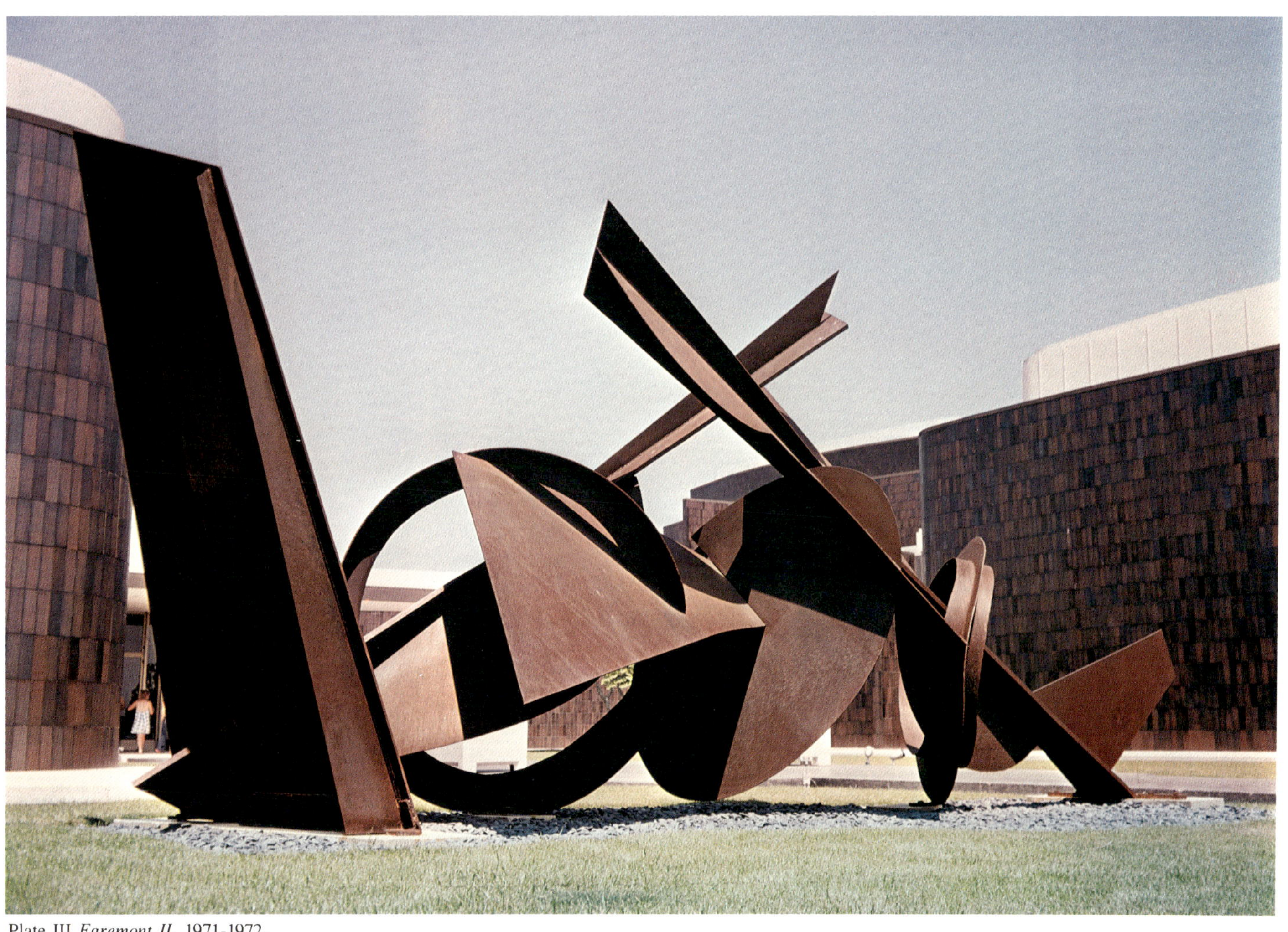

Plate III *Egremont II,* 1971-1972.
Cor-Ten steel. 144 x 240 x 144 in. (365.7 x 609.6 x 365.7 cm.)
Collection Norton Simon Museum, Pasadena, California,
Gift of Margery and Harry Kahn, 1975

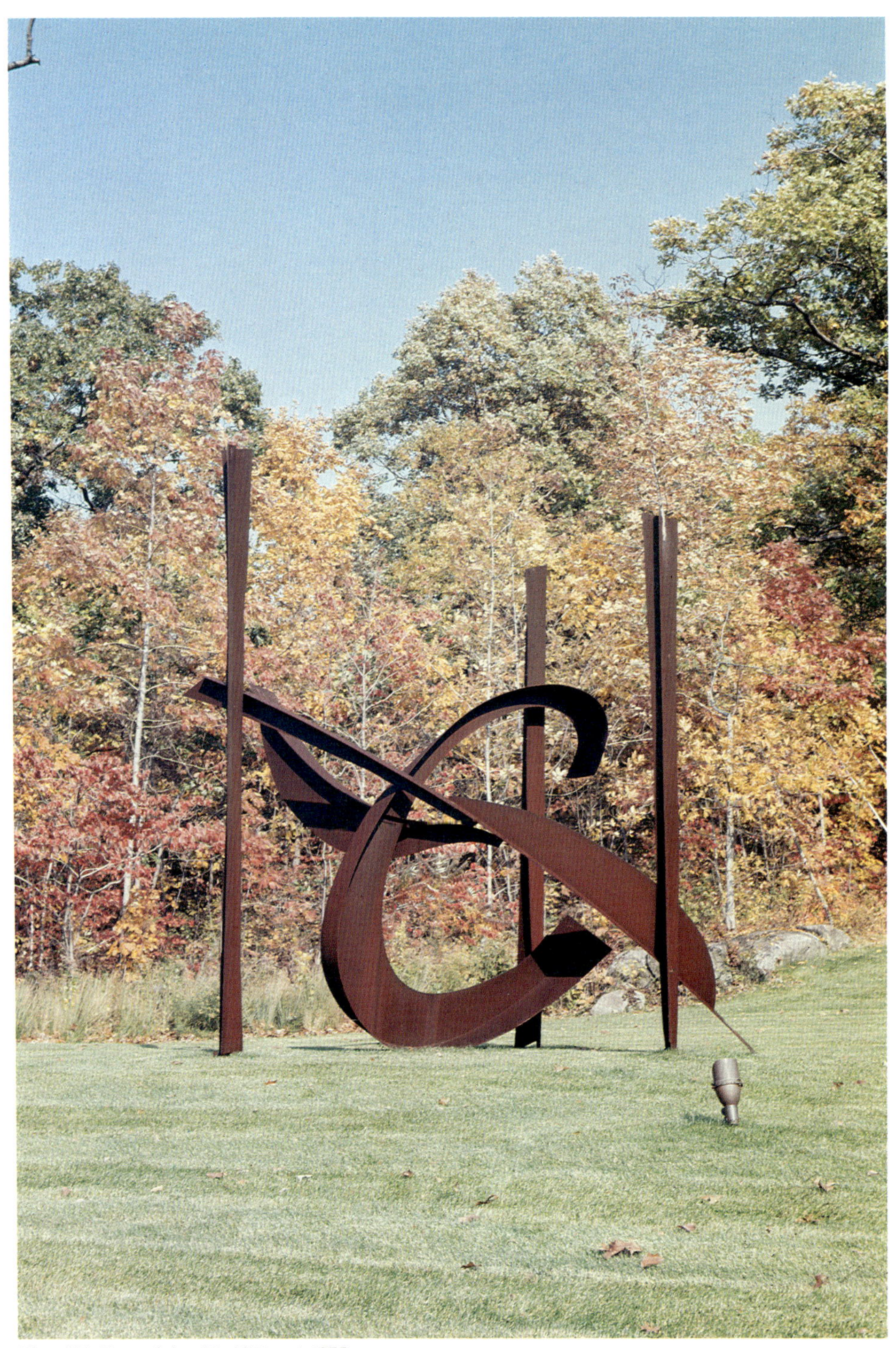

Plate IV *Three Poles III*, 1971 and 1975.
Cor-Ten steel. 180 x 144 x 180 in. (457.2 x 365.7 x 457.2 cm.)
Collection Mr. and Mrs. Milton Gilbert, Alpine, New Jersey

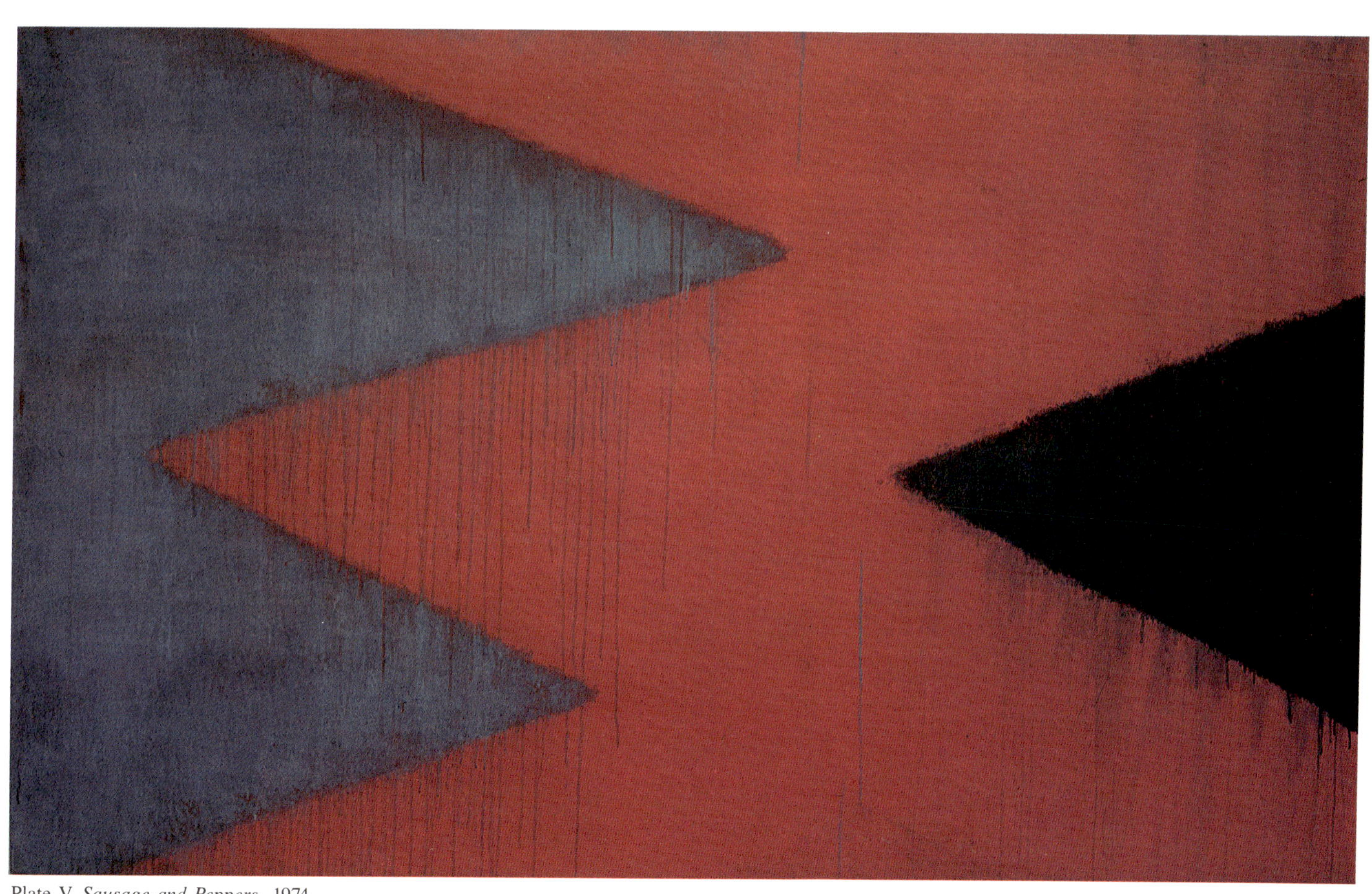

Plate V *Sausage and Peppers*, 1974.
Acrylic on canvas. 54 x 89 in. (137.1 x 226.1 cm.)
Collection Herbert Ferber,
Courtesy of M. Knoedler & Co., Inc., New York

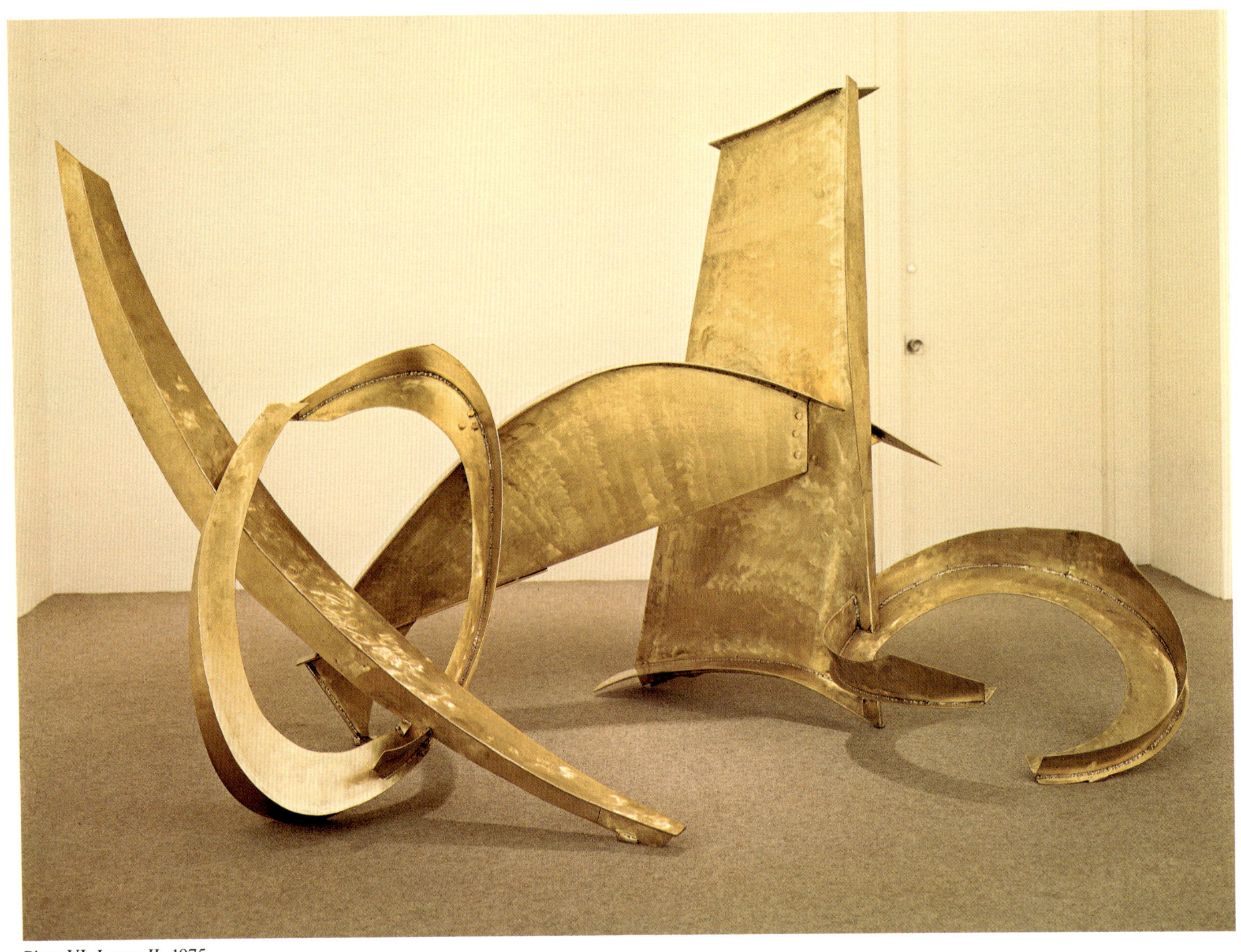

Plate VI *Lenox II*, 1975.
Brass. 72 x 120 x 72 in. (182.9 x 304.8 x 182.9 cm.)
Collection Murray Financial Corporation, Dallas

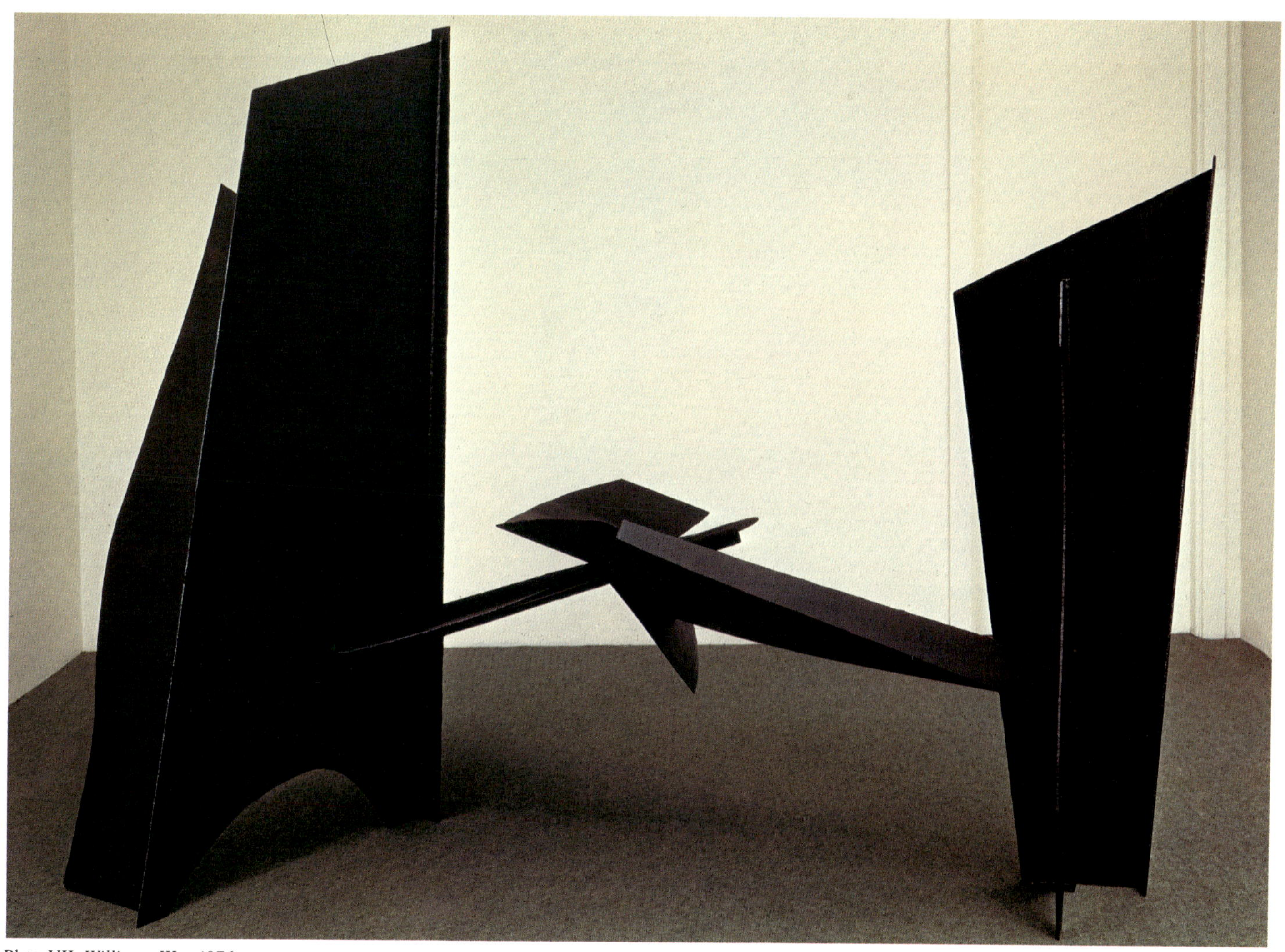

Plate VII *Williams IIIa*, 1976.
Steel. 78 x 112 x 70 in. (198.1 x 284.5 x 177.8 cm.)
Collection Herbert Ferber,
Courtesy of M. Knoedler & Co., Inc., New York

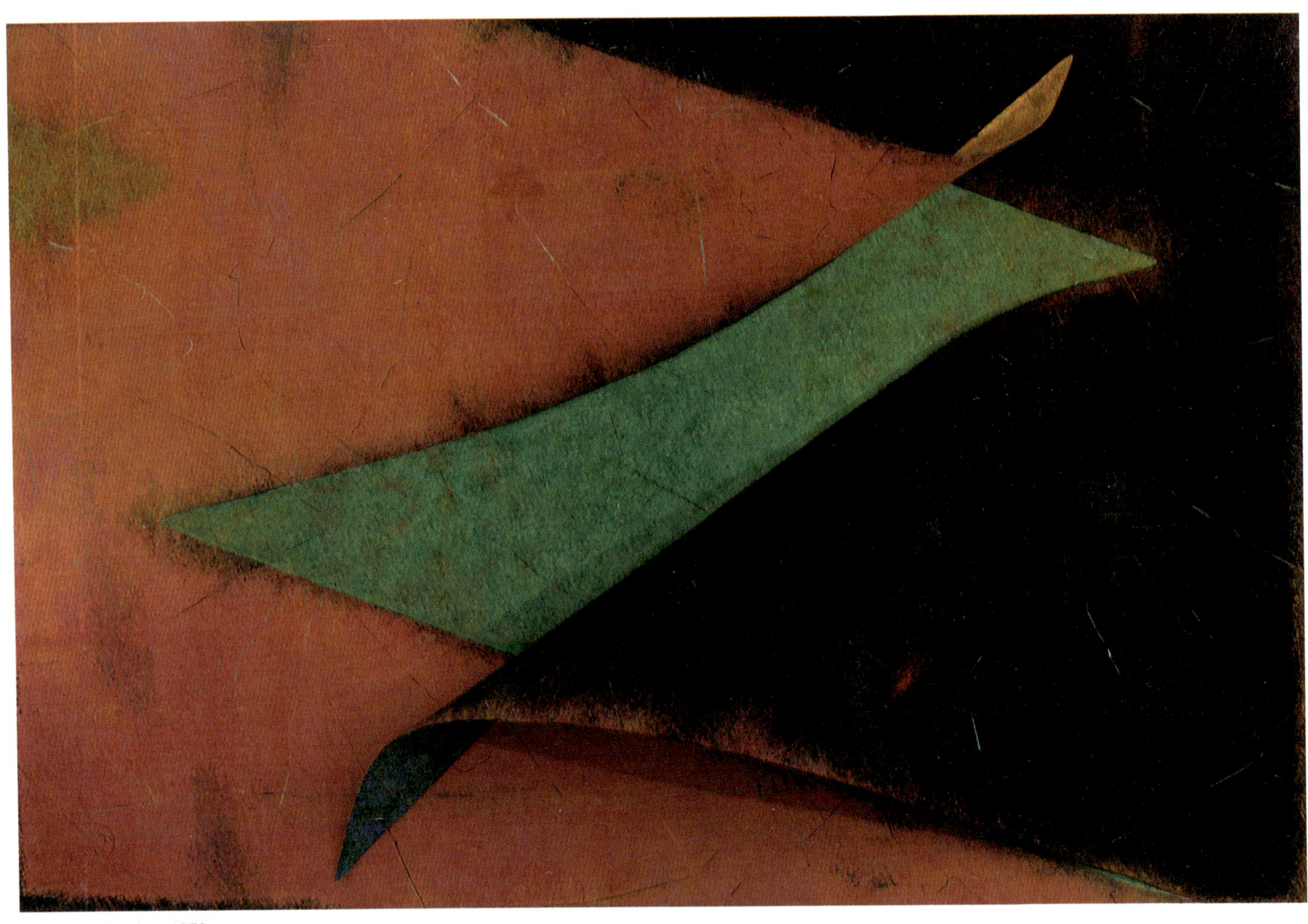

Plate VIII *Becket,* 1979.
Synthetic polymer paint on canvas. 61 x 90 x 13 in. (153 x 228.6 x 33 cm.)
Lent by Henry V. Heuser, Jr., Louisville, Kentucky

Herbert Ferber

Sculpture, Painting, Drawing 1945-1980

At the age of seventy-six, Herbert Ferber is working with the energy and intensity of a man half his age. His art shows a clarity, a confidence, and a sureness that comes only from long years of hard-won experience. What is all the more remarkable — and gratifying — is the feeling one has that he is just beginning, that there are still untapped reserves which will yield even more work at the same high level. His art has continued to renew itself in a way uncommon to the surviving members of his generation, and taken as a body, it constitutes a high achievement of post-1945 American art.

Ferber belongs artistically and chronologically to the generation that includes Jackson Pollock, Willem de Kooning, Hans Hofmann, Mark Rothko, Adolph Gottlieb, Barnett Newman, and the sculptors Alexander Calder, David Smith, David Hare, Ibram Lassaw, Theodore Roszak, and Seymour Lipton, the generation that matured in the years immediately following World War II and brought American art to a position of international prominence. With the notable exception of David Smith's (1906-1965) work, however, sculpture has not received as much attention as painting. Since 1956,[1] in fact, American sculpture of this generation has been identified almost exclusively with Smith, and after Smith's death it seemed an irrevocably closed issue. Thus we too often have missed the full significance of the sustained and high quality of Ferber's work at its best over the last thirty-five years. There can — and should — be no denying Smith's greatness, but it need not obscure other highly accomplished, if lesser-known, art of a generation that included an exceptional number of first-rate artists.

Ferber reminds one in some ways of Adolph Gottlieb and Hans Hofmann.[2] Like them he has evolved slowly and surely in an unspectacular fashion that has been all too easy to miss during the last twenty years when a higher premium has been placed on the "new" and "innovative." Ferber's art has changed and emerged gradually in an incremental, cumulative manner through a process which forces us to distinguish innovation from originality, individuality, and synthesis, as Barbara Rose remarked in another context.[3] The distinction is important, and as William Rubin noted in 1976 in his article on Ferber, "The creation of much modern art we judge to be of high quality has traditionally — and to a fault — been associated with the invention of new formal devices."[4] Rubin also notes that "even the most radical painters and sculptors participate incrementally in an ongoing tradition," adding that Ferber's art does not lend itself to instant art history. Rather, notes Rubin, he is one of those artists who "while developing and extending the collective artistic vocabulary are more concerned with the depth and sincerity of their expression than with the look of the new."[5] In hindsight, however, the lack of critical or popular acclaim perhaps has worked to his advantage, much as it did for Hofmann. Darby Bannard has pointed out that without public apotheosis, Hofmann was able to go his own way and thus kept his work from becoming pat, with no final style that could deteriorate into a mannerism.[6] We sense the same with Ferber, that he is just now at the peak of his powers.

Ferber's early career followed a course somewhat different from most other sculptors of his generation in that his im-

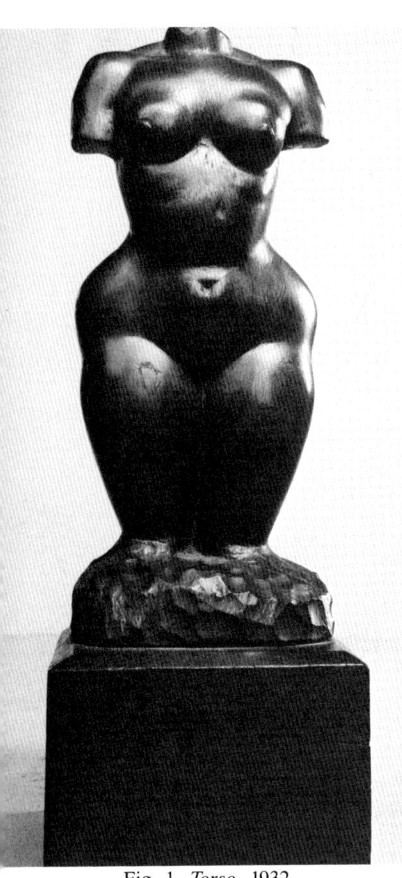

Fig. 1. *Torso*, 1932.

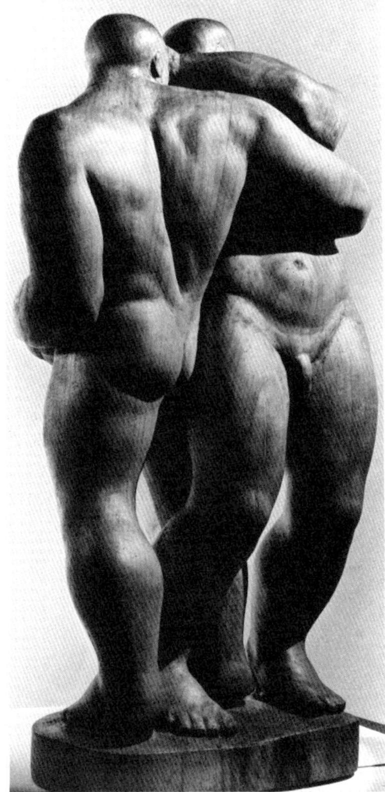

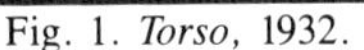

Fig. 2. *Wrestlers*, 1934.

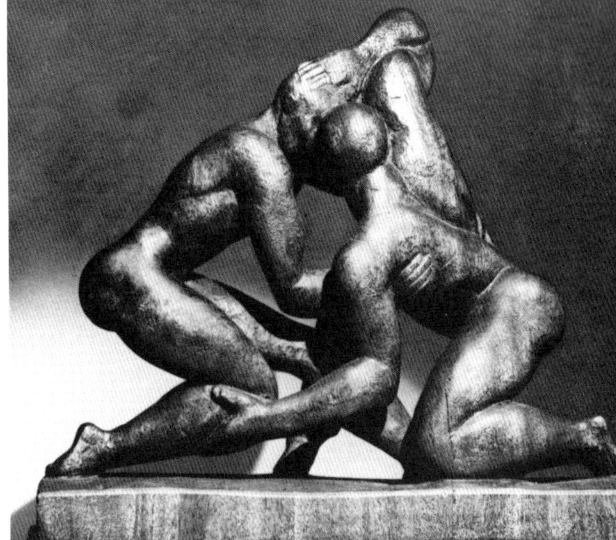

Fig. 3. *Wrestlers*, 1936.

mersion in advanced modernism was more gradual than theirs. He entered the College of the City of New York in 1923, and although he majored in science, he developed concurrently an interest in literature, philosophy, and the history of art, subjects in which he has always been articulate and well-informed. He began frequenting museums in New York. In 1926, he left CCNY by special arrangement to enter Columbia University Dental School. As part of his medical training, he was required to make anatomical drawings. (One here recalls Raymond Duchamp-Villon [1876-1918], who was also trained as a medical student before he became an artist.) He found that he had a talent for drawing and was encouraged to pursue it as an extra-academic interest. He enjoyed drawing enough so that after a year of dental school he enrolled in the Beaux Arts Institute of Design, where he attended night classes from 1927 to 1930. The institute was primarily an architectural sculpture school, and there he began serious training in sculpture and developed a lasting concern for public sculpture.[7] In 1930 he was awarded a D.D.S. from Columbia and accepted a job as a part-time dentistry instructor. At the same time he committed himself to the serious pursuit of his art, at first concentrating as much on painting and etching as on sculpture.[8]

In 1930-1931 he made his first wood carvings, guided by the example of William Zorach, the leading American exponent of the credos of direct-carve sculpture and truth to materials which were the dominant tenets of conservative American sculpture of the time. By the end of 1932, Ferber was devoting himself primarily to sculpture, and while direct carving in wood was his guiding method, Ferber was absorbing far more

than the art of Zorach and other woodcarvers such as José de Creft, Chaim Gross, and Robert Laurent. His *Torso* (fig. 1) of 1932, for example, incorporates Maillol's stable classicism and the exaggerated anatomies of Gaston Lachaise (1882-1935), America's greatest sculptor at that time. Ferber later noted that Lachaise's ability to balance a massive figure in a way that appeared to defy its weight was important to him,[9] and this quality has marked Ferber's sculpture to the present. The pose of the two interlocked figures in Ferber's *Wrestlers* of 1934 (fig. 2) recalls Maillol's *Two Female Wrestlers* of 1900 (Collection Perls Galleries, New York), and the massive figures indicate Ferber's study of the pre-Columbian art in The American Museum of Natural History in New York, a frequent haunt in the thirties and forties. He also became deeply interested in African sculpture through visits to the Guillaume collection made as early as 1930 and through his own collecting in the field which he began a year later. The power and clarity of primitive art appealed to him, because it paralleled the aesthetic ends of direct-carve sculpture, as did the similar qualities of the medieval — especially Romanesque — sculpture he had seen at The Metropolitan Museum of Art, in reproductions, and in the George Grey Barnard Collection.[10] At the same time, the art of these cultures also demonstrated new possibilities for a more Expressionist direction, a shift that his work took after 1934.

The heavy-set figures of the 1934 *Wrestlers* also reveal an awareness of the socially oriented sculpture of Ernst Barlach, an indication of Ferber's growing concern with social-realist themes, here rendered as a metaphor of the human struggle caused by the turbulent political, social, and economic condi-

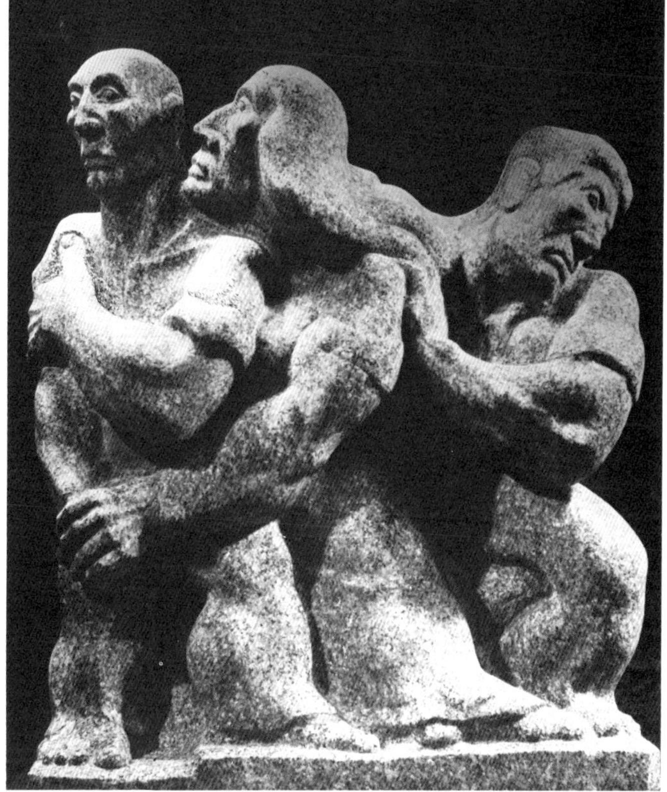

Fig. 4. *To Fight Again*, 1937.

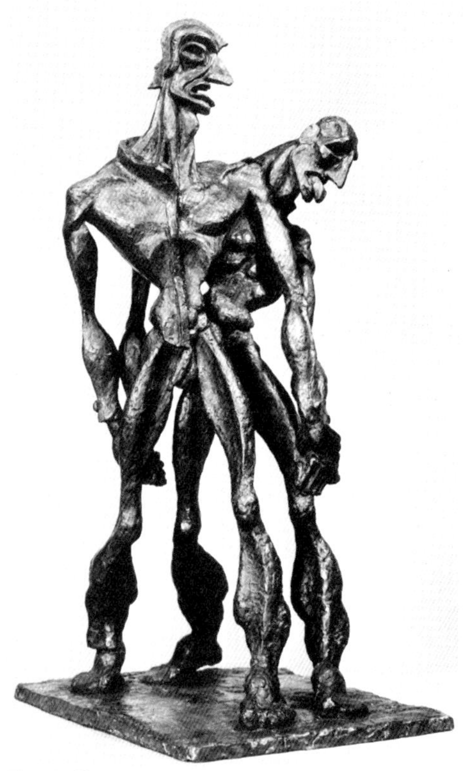

Fig. 5. *Shadow of a Hero*, 1943.

tions of the 1930s. His sensitivity to social causes is echoed in his 1936 sculpture of the same title (fig. 3). Here, though, the kneeling figures are interlocked in an exacting geometric balance which recalls the pose and attitude of the two figures in Maillol's relief *Desire*, 1906-1908, which entered the collection of The Museum of Modern Art, New York, in 1930. Ferber's growing respect for Romanesque sculpture (comparable to Duchamp-Villon's love of the Gothic) is manifested here in the parallel between the intricate configurations of the wrestlers and the composition of a Romanesque capital relief. The social-realist tenor of his art was intensified in 1936. He joined a John Reed Club and the Artist's Union, where he attended talks given by the Mexican muralists Orozco and Siqueiros, who were visiting New York to promulgate social-realist art. Ferber's *To Fight Again* (fig. 4) of 1936-1937 reflects these concerns as well as the mood of suffering found in the art of Käthe Kollwitz, whose importance to him at this time Ferber has acknowledged.[11] By 1938, however, Ferber became disillusioned with Stalin and began to disengage himself from the activities of the John Reed Club and the Artist's Union.[12] However, social-realist themes, rendered in a more metaphorical guise, continued to appear in his work for some years to come.

In the summer of 1938 he travelled in Europe for two months and gained his first experience of art outside New York and the social-realist milieu. He visited as many cathedrals as possible in France and Italy, and his direct, sustained experience of Romanesque sculpture, especially at Moissac, Souillac, and Carcassone, confirmed and quickened the shift to more predominantly Expressionist sculpture that he had

begun four years earlier. From 1938 until 1945 his work was deeply shaped by the distortions of what he later termed the "false perspective" of Romanesque capitals.[13] The attenuation of the sculptures at Souillac and Moissac, as well as those of African art, offered potent examples of an expansive sculpture that went beyond the inert density of the traditional carved monolith — a "sculpture of surface," as Ferber termed it.[14] By 1940 he saw this as limiting and thus for him closed to further productive exploration.

In his search for ways to move beyond the monolith, Ferber found an example in the Expressionist sculpture of Ossip Zadkine, whose thinned, loosely modelled work had been exhibited in New York in 1937 at the Brummer Gallery and at the Curt Valentin Gallery in 1943 after Zadkine had fled the war and immigrated to the United States. In Ferber's *Shadow of a Hero* (fig. 5) of 1943, the old mood of social concern was intensified by the crisis atmosphere of the world war in much the same way as Zadkine's work was at the time. More tellingly, like Zadkine's, the figures were modelled in bronze, rather than carved in wood or stone, and the outlines were stretched, pulled, and radically distorted by the hand. The concave and convex planes and cavities move rapidly and continuously, dissolving the former hegemony of the solid block. Here and in *Reclining Woman I* (fig. 6) of 1944-1945, mass and weight have been reduced drastically, and the figure pulls away from the solid monolithic core. But this type of Expressionist sculpture, to Ferber's eye, also verged on a total dissolution of the underlying formal structure he found unsatisfactory and soon abandoned.

In 1944 he came under the strong influence of Henry

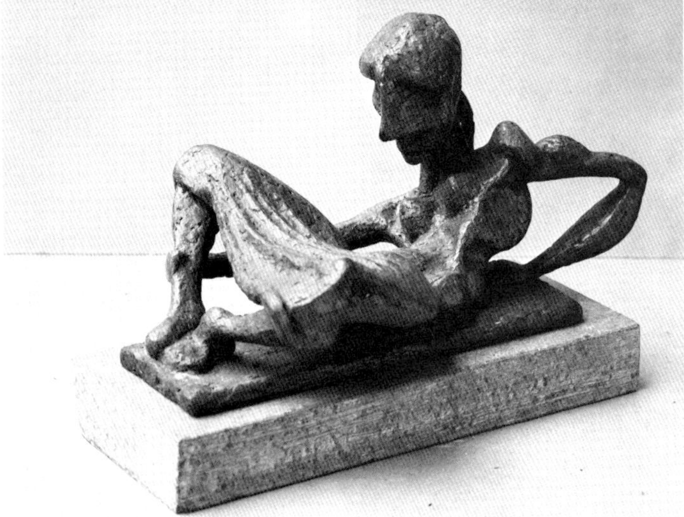

Fig. 6. *Reclining Woman I*, 1944.

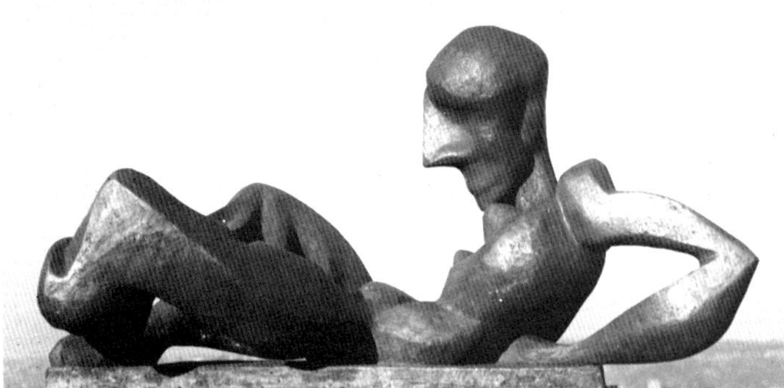

Fig. 7. *Reclining Woman II*, 1945.

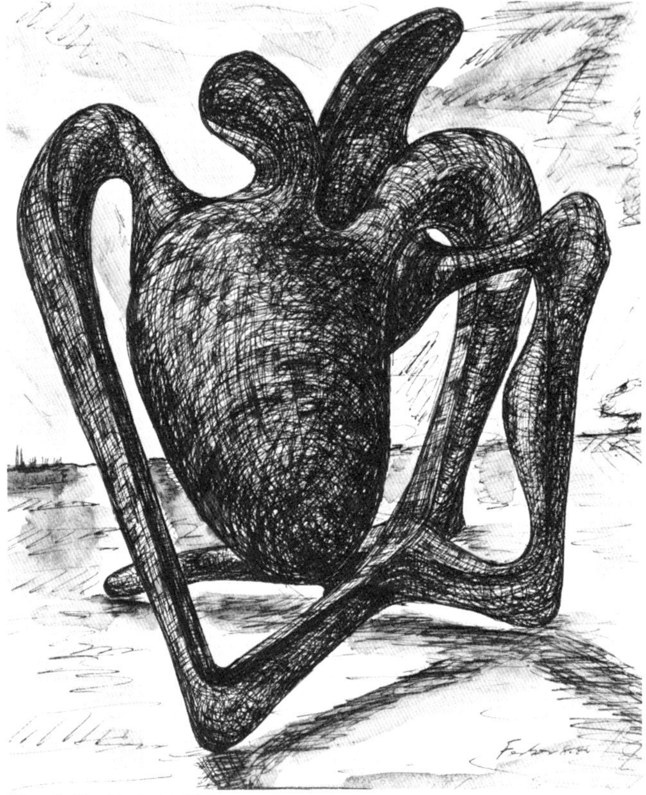

Fig. 8. Untitled, 1946.

Moore, who had shown for some years at the Curt Valentin Gallery. In 1944 Valentin also had published a large volume on Moore that contained over 200 reproductions of Moore's sculpture and drawing, a book that became an essential guide for Ferber in 1944-1945.[15] His example gave Ferber a new and surer sense of direction, but Moore's influence was so intense that for almost a year Ferber did little sculpture, realizing that anything he did would look too much like Moore's. Ferber's *Reclining Woman II* (fig. 7) of 1945, one of the few sculptures he did at this time, confirms this observation. Ferber concentrated instead on drawing and produced hundreds of drawings which explored the formal, thematic implications suggested by Moore's work. Through Moore, Ferber found the means to shift from the figurative basis that had formed his art to a sculpture that was more thoroughly abstract in both conception and execution. Once he established an abstract basis for his sculpture, Ferber became increasingly interested in achieving an "extension and thinness"[16] that would ultimately take him to a complete remove from the monolithic block he had worked with for so long. The intensive drawing process he underwent also demonstrated the myriad possibilities inherent in an abstract art.

Drawing, both as a process and as the technique of shaping forms, has remained essential to him to this day. Since the 1940s, Ferber has been a compulsive draftsman, and his working method has always been based on one or more drawings in which he conceives and then develops the ideas for the sculpture. The drawings usually are full-blown wash drawings (and thus are often more like small paintings) which generally are set in a vast landscape, as were Moore's drawings of the late

1930s. The empty, imaginary spaces of the landscape setting, in both Ferber and Moore's work, recall the hallucinatory spaces of de Chirico and the illusionist Surrealists (fig. 8).

Although Moore had pierced and opened the monolith to some extent, Ferber needed a different type of sculpture to achieve the abstract art of extension and thinness that he now envisioned.[17] He required the open constructed sculpture invented by Picasso in 1912 and more fully developed by the collaboration of Picasso and Julio Gonzalez in the late 1920s. It had been adopted by many sculptors of Ferber's generation, and over the next several years Ferber incorporated its techniques in his own work. Fundamental to this development were the examples offered by, first, the "transparent" sculptures begun by Jacques Lipchitz in the 1920s and by Gonzalez, whose *Head* (Collection The Museum of Modern Art, New York) of 1935 Ferber had seen at The Museum of Modern Art. As we shall see, Picasso's Surrealist paintings and, in particular, the drawing of Joan Miró especially were important.

Miró and Surrealist drawing, for example, enabled Ferber to loosen and open up his shapes and to free himself from a specific, literal image and move toward a formal simplification and fluency. The effects were seen in *Three-Legged Woman II* (fig. 9) of late 1945, which marked the emergence of Ferber's personal and mature style. The title suggests a hybrid Surrealist creature, indicating the intensity of the Surrealist milieu in New York that Ferber had begun to absorb by this time. The piece is characterized by a free-flowing, continuous line delineating a biomorphic form language that synthesized, in addition to Miró, elements of Arp, the early Giacometti, and Lipchitz. Also apparent are overtones of the

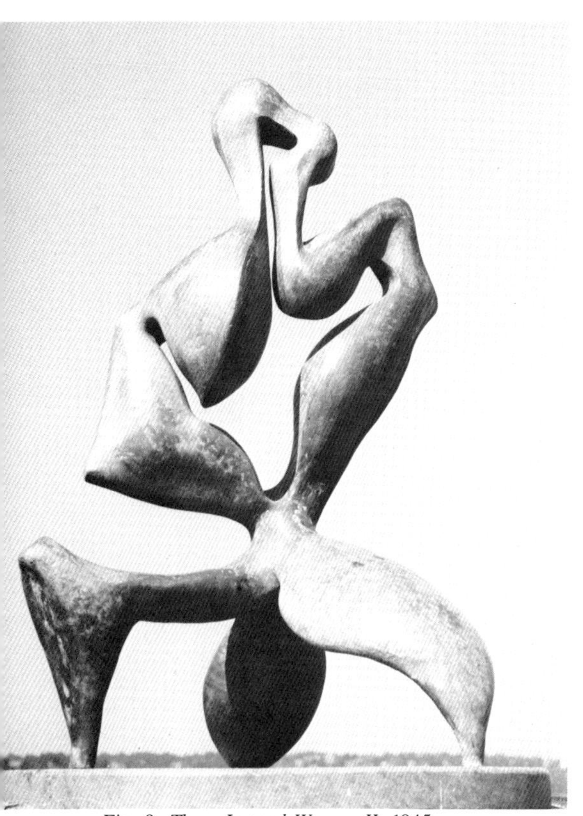

Fig. 9. *Three-Legged Woman II*, 1945.

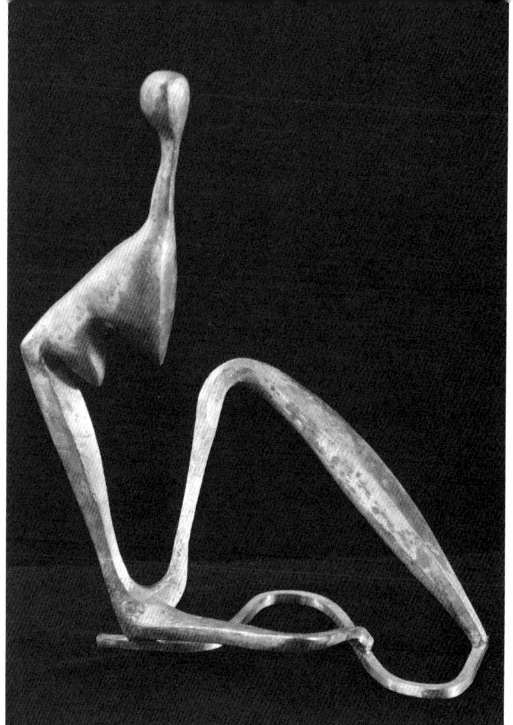

Fig. 10. *Seated Figure*, 1945.

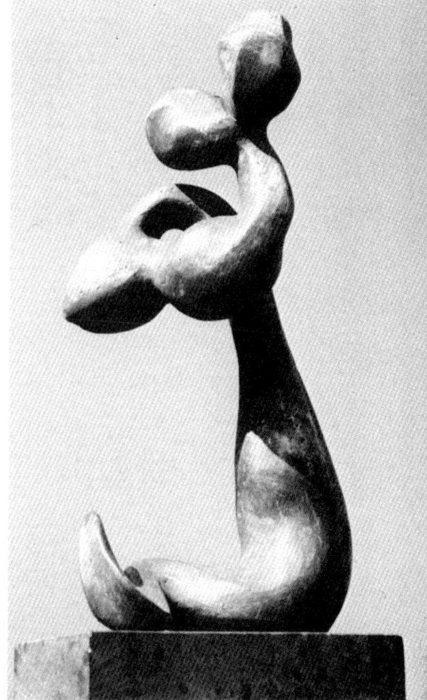

Fig. 11. *Mermaid*, 1946.

distorted anatomies of Picasso's bathers of the late 1920s. These sources assisted Ferber in realizing several of the formal ends of the open sculpture he was seeking; the sculpture no longer displaces space so much as it moves and extends itself in and through space, with space now incorporated as an active formal agent. Further, the sculpture is no longer anchored to the base as a heavy mass but begins to elevate itself, touching and supporting itself on multiple points, imparting a sense of weightlessness or at least lightness, all characteristics that have remained at the very heart of Ferber's work to the present.[18]

The sculpture produced by American artists of Ferber's generation after 1945 often has been characterized as "drawing in space," a description first applied to the new open sculpture by Gonzalez in referring to Picasso's welded iron work.[19] The term is apt in that it suggests the formal powers of invention that were made possible through a thin, linear metal sculpture. However, it is inaccurate, because the three dimensions of sculpture only can be brought into existence slowly and painstakingly by processes which are antithetical to the immediacy of drawing. To preserve as much of the sense of immediacy as possible, Ferber began to work with direct metal processes, as had the other sculptors of his generation, starting with Alexander Calder and David Smith as early as 1931 and 1932.[20] The *Three-Legged Woman* was Ferber's first work in direct metal, using lead because of its softness and pliability. He worked with a gas torch hooked up to the kitchen stove and used repoussé sheets of 1/8-inch lead soldered at the edges to make hollow forms which were reinforced inside with an armature of brass rods. It gave Ferber the technical impetus

he needed, but he soon found lead too soft and too weak to maintain its shape. In 1949 he turned to the blowtorch to solder copper and brass. Only in 1954 did he begin to use the oxyacetylene torch for welding steel and brass.

Ferber never has considered materials and techniques as an end in themselves, believing that ideas, not materials, make art. He has spoken often and strongly against the danger of making a fetish of materials, which he felt was an objectionable characteristic of the Bauhaus and which probably was also a reaction against the truth-to-materials dogma of the thirties.[21] In fact, once he had established full technical control of the open-sculpture idiom, Ferber did not hesitate to cast his pieces in bronze from plaster models in order to gain the strength and support this type of work required. For Ferber, finding the material appropriate and necessary to execute the idea was the key to creating original works of art.

Ferber's process also is traditional in that, as noted, he begins with one or more drawings. He then makes a small version or working model and finally moves to the larger, definitive sculpture. Formal changes and adjustments for scale are made throughout the process. The *Three-Legged Woman*, for example, was done first in a version eleven inches high before it was enlarged to a height of two feet.

With a personal breakthrough achieved in this work, Ferber gained a new fluency and mastery of line and devised more inventive configurations in the *Seated Figure* (fig. 10) of late 1945 and *Mermaid* (fig. 11) of 1946, works that recall organic elements in Miró's paintings of women done in the early thirties. The upper portion of Picasso's 1930 *Seated Bather* (Collection The Museum of Modern Art, New York)

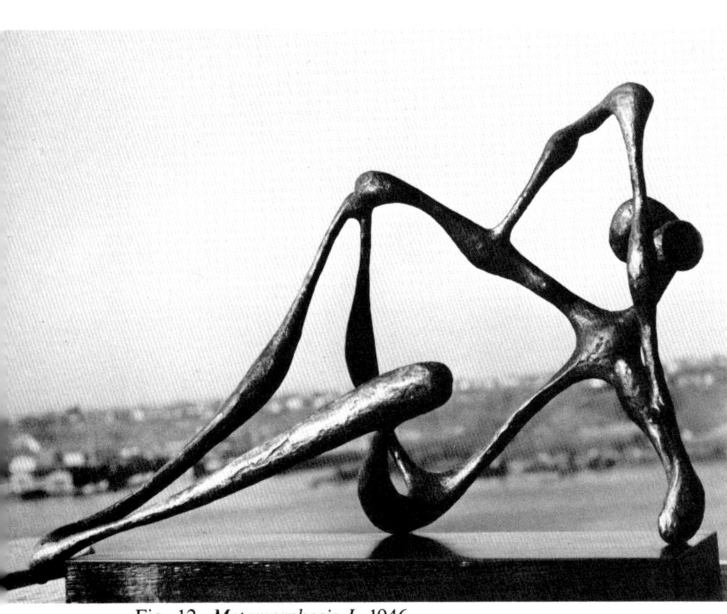

Fig. 12. *Metamorphosis I*, 1946.

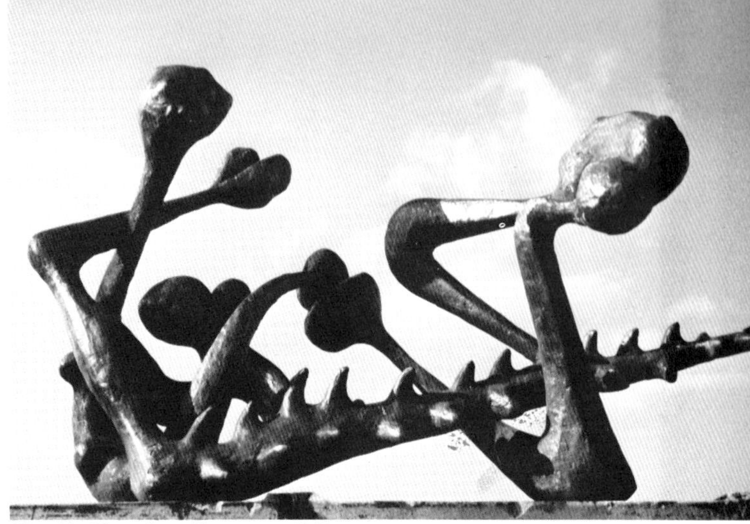

Fig. 14. *Hazardous Encounter*, 1947.

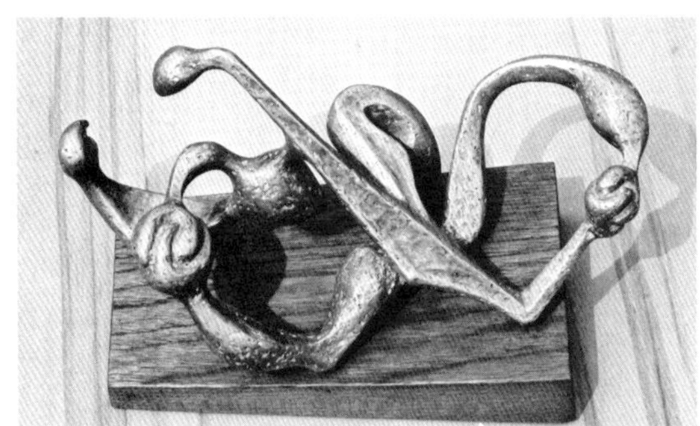

Fig. 13. *Act of Aggression II*, 1946.

also may have been a source for *Mermaid*. Clearly, the two Spanish masters were crucial models for Ferber. Picasso was a hero to Ferber because through his artistic powers Picasso could absorb all art history, turning it to his own uses and thus moving his art into new realms unknown to American art. So, too, Ferber looked to Picasso's commitment to art as a way of life as an important example. Ferber felt this type of total commitment was a necessary but difficult condition for the artist to achieve in America.[22] Most immediately, he owed to Picasso the conception of sculpture that allowed him to achieve the thinness and extension in space he was seeking. Finally, Picasso offered a rich, pervasive formal language that offered Ferber and virtually every artist of his generation an unending source of exploration.

Ferber also quickly developed a great admiration for Miró,[23] whose powers of invention, realized through an autonomy of line, offered boundless formal possibilities. Calder's debt to Miró has been well-documented,[24] but the full extent of Miró's influence on American art only now is becoming better-known. For Ferber and virtually every other artist of his generation, Miró was as important as Picasso in shaping their art.[25] Miró's stature in America was established fully by his retrospective at The Museum of Modern Art in 1941, and his new work was readily accessible in depth at exhibitions held virtually every year after 1945 at the Pierre Matisse Gallery. Ferber made a special point of meeting Miró in 1947 when he was in New York to paint the large mural that was installed later at the Terrace Plaza Hotel in Cincinnati.[26] Ferber still strongly feels Miró's presence daily through three works on paper which hang in his home. Miró's liberating

drawing was one of the most important catalysts for the actual achievement of Ferber's first mature sculptures of 1945-1947. To a great extent, the examples of Picasso and Miró enabled Ferber to move beyond the confines of the carver and modeller and embrace fully the international tradition of modern art.

The importance of Ferber's own drawing process and the paintings of Miró and Picasso indicate that Ferber, Calder, Smith, and others of his generation no longer made a rigid distinction between painting and sculpture. Rather, they envisioned an ideal aesthetic order wherein painting and sculpture would be fused in a common form language, with "the only difference being the material use of a dimension, in place of an indicated one," as Smith had defined it in 1940.[27] Ferber, Smith, Calder, and Roszak began as painters before turning to sculpture, which gave the impetus to break down the old barriers between the two media. Calder had combined elements from the painting of Miró and Mondrian in 1930-1931 in his first stabiles, and David Smith's initial sculptures grew out from the painting surface when he applied three-dimensional objects directly to the canvas, establishing the pattern for Roszak, Ferber, and others who followed.[28] Ferber also viewed the work of Arp and Ernst as important examples in this regard. Ferber in a very real sense has never stopped painting, thus ensuring a continuing and easy dialogue between the two media in his work. As we shall see, the fusion of painting and sculpture has shaped significantly the character and quality of Ferber's art.

In *Metamorphosis I*, (fig. 12), 1946, which carries the same title but no formal similarity to Picasso's and André Masson's sculptures of 1928, Ferber attained a new degree of

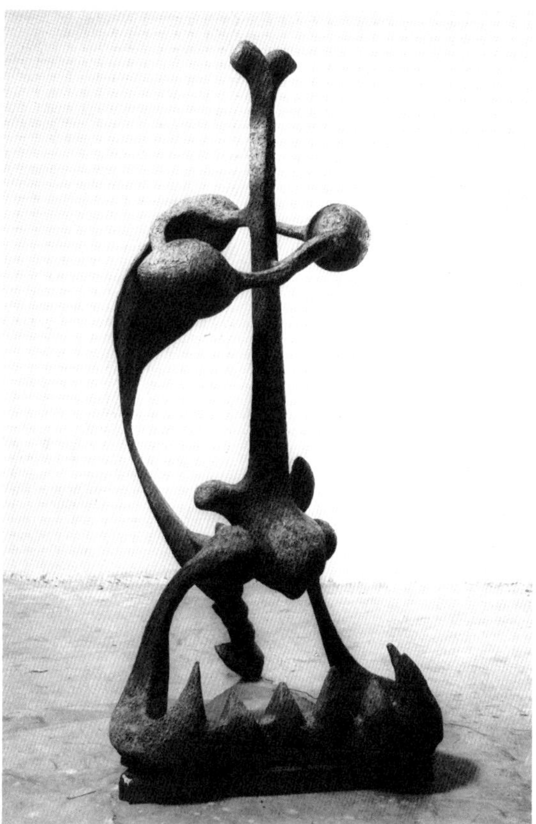

Fig. 15. *Surrational Zeus II*, 1947.

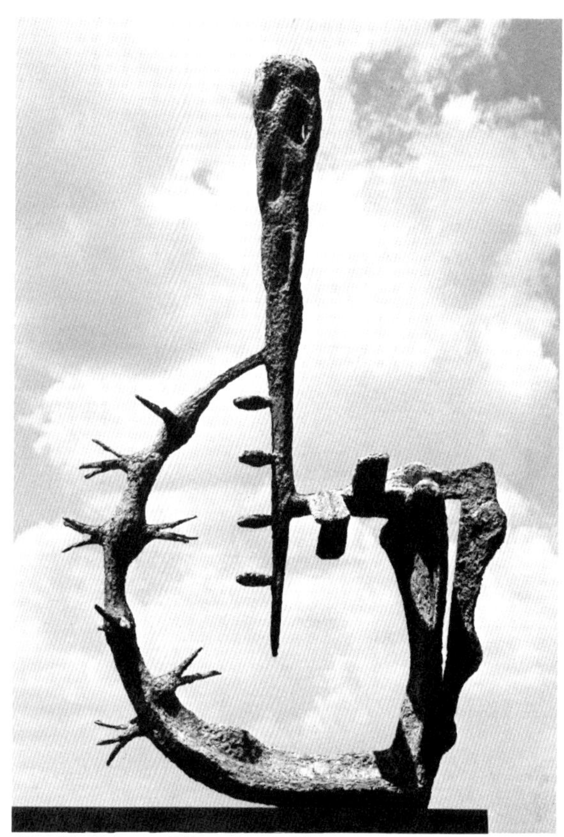

Fig. 16. *Labors of Hercules*, 1948.

openness and thinness in his sculpture. Nevertheless, because of its continuous, flowing line, this work seems to delineate, if not actually to enclose, the three dimensions of the human body. (In fact, the sculpture was the culminating piece in the *Reclining Woman* series begun two years earlier.) To discard these last references to mass and three dimensions, Ferber thereafter obliterated the continuous line and shifted to sculpture composed of disparate, separate parts defined by fragmented segments of line.[29] This shift would account for a new degree of tension within the sculpture itself and for a more powerful extension of the parts in space, two formal objectives which were now paramount to Ferber's approach. The change was first evident in *Act of Aggression II* (fig. 13), in which the generalized form language of the earlier biomorphism was transformed into intensely personal, deeply emotive, and often violent themes and configurations of a type that would characterize his work for the next two years. The sculpture owes a strong debt to Giacometti's *Woman with Her Throat Cut* (Collection The Museum of Modern Art, New York) of 1932, both for its low-lying lateral posture and the violent tenor, but the theme of struggle ultimately can be traced to Ferber's *Wrestlers* of 1934.[30]

The progressive intensity of his work at this time stemmed from the heightened influence of what he termed the "unmasked emotions"[31] of Surrealism in which he had become deeply involved. His full immersion in the personal and poetic world of Surrealism in late 1946 was propelled by his contact with the artists of the Betty Parsons Gallery, which he joined that year. These artists and those from the adjacent Kootz Gallery included Jackson Pollock, Adolph Gottlieb, Robert Mother-

well, William Baziotes, Bradley Walker Tomlin, Theodore Stamos, Barnett Newman, and Mark Rothko, who all were exploring the themes and techniques of Surrealism and turning them to their own pictorial ends. Ferber became close friends with the members of the group, especially with Rothko, and participated actively in countless meetings and gatherings. These meetings often were held at Ferber's house, and the group would discuss art, its sources, its purposes, its making fervently for hours. The interchange with fellow members was close and intense, and Ferber remembers Newman visiting his studio and discussing a single piece of Ferber's for several hours.[32]

Using the examples of Picasso, Miró, and to a lesser degree Arp, Masson, Matta, and Ernst, Ferber and the rest of the group focused on transforming Surrealist ideas concerning the unconscious, private realities and impulses, and mythological symbols into concrete plastic structures which contained multiple and ambiguous meanings. Their work was permeated with themes which emphasized psychic experience as transmitted through the primordial, the mythic, and ritual acts referring to the drama of birth, death, war, and sexuality. Such layers of multiple associations were viewed as appropriate personal expressions of the prevailing mood of uncertainty, irrationality, and personal angst induced by the trauma of the newborn nuclear age. The extreme emotional intensity with which Ferber approached his art at this time was captured by his evocative statement in 1947:

The artist must actually crawl over every square inch of his work, touching, smearing, retouching, licking and spitting,

15

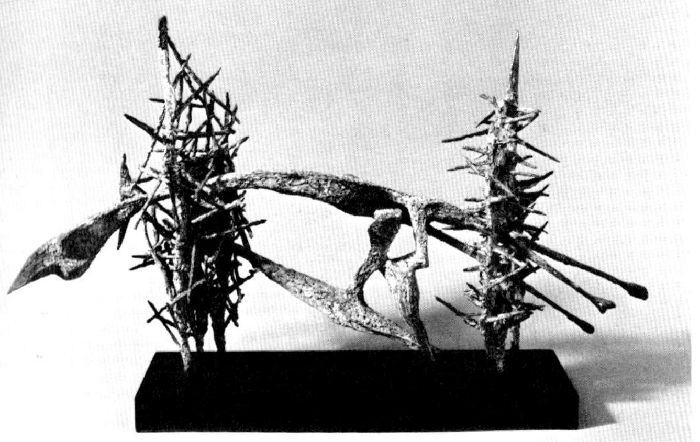

Fig. 17. *Jackson Pollock*, 1949.

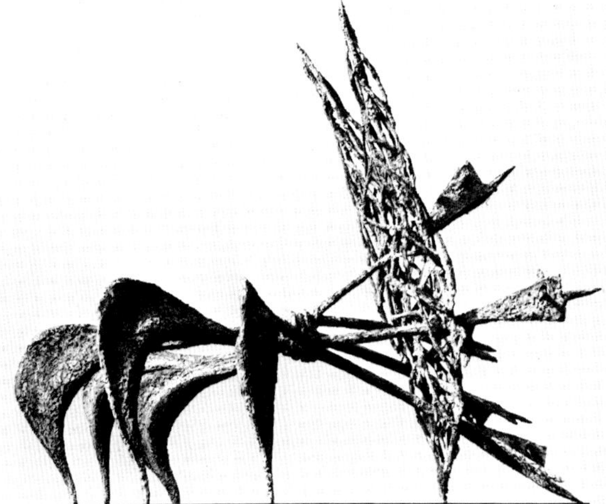

Fig. 18. *Manifestation II*, 1949.

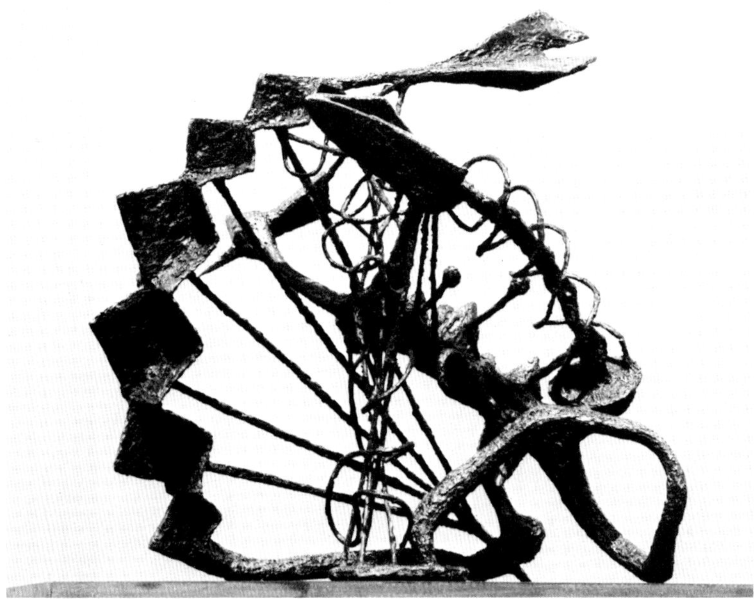

Fig. 19. *The Action is the Pattern*, 1949.

expending himself over the whole thing and forcing it bit by bit to become in an intimate and immediate way, himself.[33]

Hazardous Encounter (fig. 14) of 1947 refers to acts of love and to threatening interpersonal contacts. It is constructed with a series of menacing forms that include references to bones, teeth, limbs, fists, joints, and a phallus-sword. As Wayne Andersen has noted, the configuration recalls Picasso's abstract anatomies of 1933.[34] Ferber in December 1947 characterized the internal drama and formal ends of this and other works of the time:

The sculptor is too often seduced by form; space is the unlimit of his medium. Surrational space, charged with form, sprung, tense as a steel coil, from those layers of being not subject to the censorship of versimilitude. . . . Space and form take shape concommitantly in creating an arena where the creative personality of the artist is in anxious conjunction with his perception of the world around him.[35]

Ferber became intimate friends with Mark Rothko and Adolph Gottlieb, two artists whose interest in mythology Ferber came to share, as in his *Surrational Zeus II* (fig. 15), *Phoenix* of 1947 (Collection of the Artist) and *Labors of Hercules* (fig. 16) of 1948. Rothko's 1944-1946 Surrealist paintings contain a type of imagery that appears to have helped spur Ferber's work at this time. For example, the theme of the enclosure of the vertical form in *Surrational Zeus II* is shared by Rothko's painting of 1946 *The Entombment*, which Ferber owned, having traded one of his own works to Rothko. The "ball-and-socket"[36] motif encircling itself at the top central portion of *The Entombment* derives from the common Surrealist motif of the mate devouring the lover in the sexual act. It also occurs in Ferber's 1947 *Apocalyptic Rider* (Collection Grey Art Gallery, New York University), but the ultimate source is Picasso's *Woman with Stiletto* (Collection Musée Picasso, Paris) of 1931 and *Seated Bather* (Collection The Museum of Modern Art, New York) of 1930.

Analogies between Ferber's skeletal drawing in the 1948 *Portrait of David Hare* (Private Collection, New York) and *Portrait of Barnett Newman* (Private Collection, New York) and Rothko's darting line in his paintings of these years also are worth noting. Ferber's admiration for Miró (shared by Rothko) was evident in the Newman portrait, which is striking because of its similarity to the "duck"-like creature in the left center of Miró's *The Tilled Field* (Collection The Solomon R. Guggenheim Museum, New York) of 1923-1924. At the same time, however, the vertical bone shape reminds one of similar elements in Arshile Gorky's *The Betrothal* (Collection Whitney Museum of American Art, New York) of 1947. These relationships, however, are significant only insofar as they demonstrate the giant steps which had been taken by these artists toward a common language shared by painting and sculpture, a language that has since been extended and amplified by Ferber and the other artists of his generation.

The bones and "teeth" of *Surrational Zeus II* and the jagged and barbed vertebrae[37] of *Hazardous Encounter* and *Portrait of David Hare* all appear to refer to prehistoric creatures. These references are made more explicit in *Portrait of Barnett Newman* and *Dragon* (Collection Edith Ferber, New York), both of which can be read as composite skeletal animals or birds, keeping in mind that the titles were assigned only after

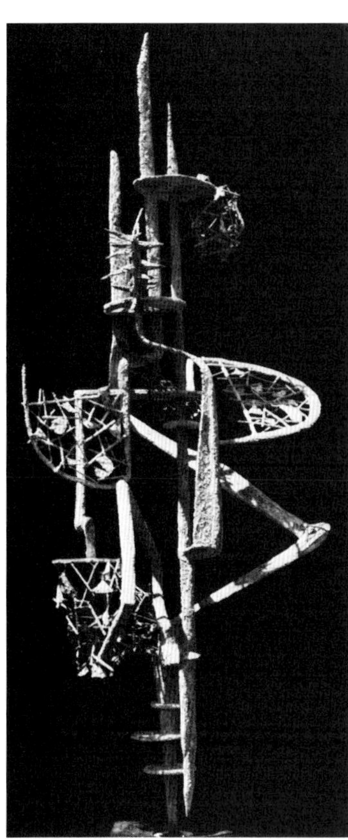

Fig. 20. *Flame*, 1949.

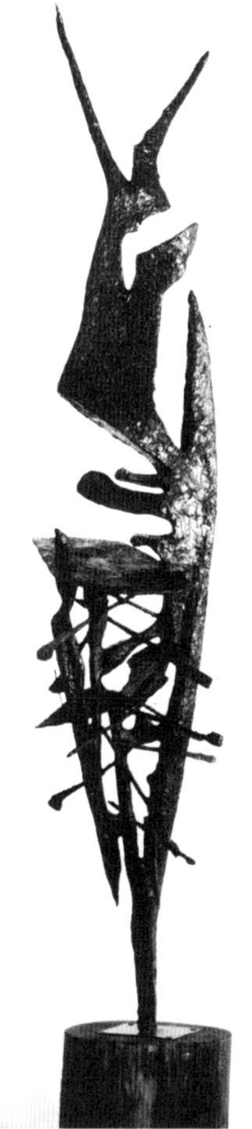

Fig. 21. *Horned Sculpture*, 1949 and 1957.

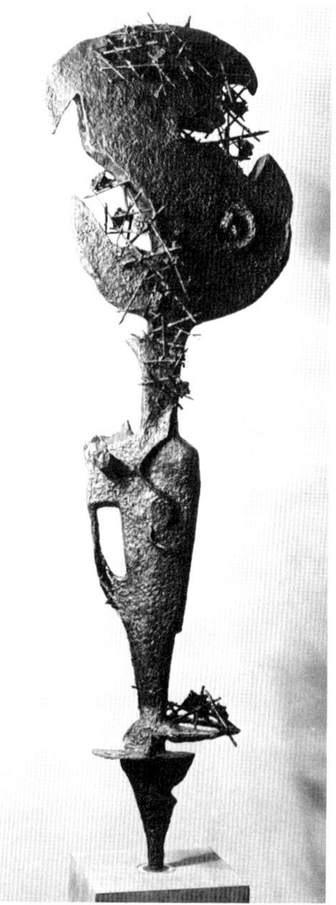

Fig. 22. *He is Not a Man*, 1950.

the works were completed. In the *Jackson Pollock* (fig. 17) of 1949, the horizontal shape is clearly a skeletal prehistoric bird,[38] and variations of a bird's head also are evident in *Manifestation II* (fig. 18) and *The Action Is the Pattern* (fig. 19), both of 1949. This image can be related to similar iconography in post-war sculpture such as Roszak's 1946 *Spectre of Kitty Hawk* (Collection The Museum of Modern Art, New York) and especially David Smith's *Jurassic Bird* (Collection Dr. and Mrs. Paul T. Makler, Philadelphia), 1945, and *Royal Bird* (Collection Walker Art Center, Minneapolis), 1948. The bird's head in Ferber's pieces also might be compared with both the claw shape at top center and the "beak" at right in Rothko's *The Entombment*. For Smith, the bird is both regal and predatory, powerful and threatening; Ferber's image, by contrast, is of a bird that has been trapped and rendered helpless by the entangling brambles and thickets. Smith's source for *Jurassic Bird* was the skeleton of a prehistoric diving bird in The American Museum of Natural History in New York.[39] As noted earlier, Ferber frequently visited the museum and "knew it well,"[40] but his familiarity with bones and skeletal structures dates from his thorough grounding in anatomy as a medical student. Ferber used this knowledge to imbue his art with a powerful sense of drama associated with birth, growth, and death, the very processes of life itself.

By 1947, following the lead of Jackson Pollock's classic all-over drip paintings, painting had begun instead to purge itself of high-pitched, literal Surrealist drama. It had begun to move to a more formal, abstract type of picture that nevertheless retained a pervasive poetic atmosphere and mood. Sculpture began to follow suit in 1949, a process that was stepped

up by Ferber, Smith, and the others of the group in 1950. However, Ferber substantially completed this process in his work only in 1952, and vestiges of his earlier style were to remain until 1956-1957. *Manifestation II* and *The Action Is the Pattern* are charged with expressive forces, but the first stage in the development of a more formal sculpture is evident in the regular, almost geometric spacing of the structural "ribs." In *The Action Is the Pattern* these "ribs," or "spokes," emanate from a central focal point at the base and connect with the surrounding edges which enclose the space. This creates the first example in his work of a spatial frame that acknowledges Constructivist sculpture,[41] in this case notably that of Naum Gabo in works such as *Spiral Theme* (Collection The Museum of Modern Art, New York) of 1941. An overriding and contrasting organic quality is evident, however, in the thrust of the "bird" head and in the lines of "rope" that twist and coil along two of the enclosing edges. This was Ferber's first fusion of the organic and the geometric, of the biomorphic and the Constructivist, a course which Wayne Andersen has outlined in detail and which had been established as a primary characteristic of American sculpture as early as 1931.[42] Briefly summarized, in that year Calder combined the biomorphism of Miró and Arp with the geometry of Mondrian and Constructivism. A similar union followed rapidly in the work of Smith, Isamu Noguchi, Ibram Lassaw, and others during the thirties and forties. Nor was it limited to sculpture. Following Picasso's lead, Gorky had synthesized Miró and Surrealism with Cubism in the thirties, and Bolotowsky had joined Miró with Mondrian in his 1936-1937 paintings such as *Abstraction No. 3* (Collection Museum of Art, Carnegie Insti-

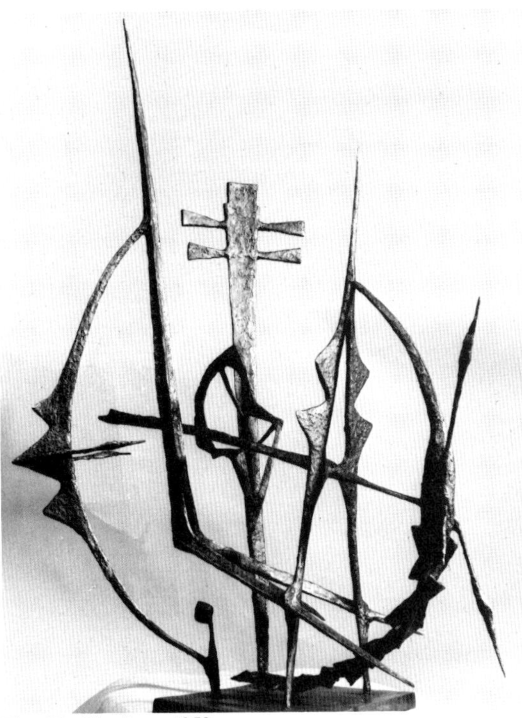

Fig. 23. *The Bow*, 1950.

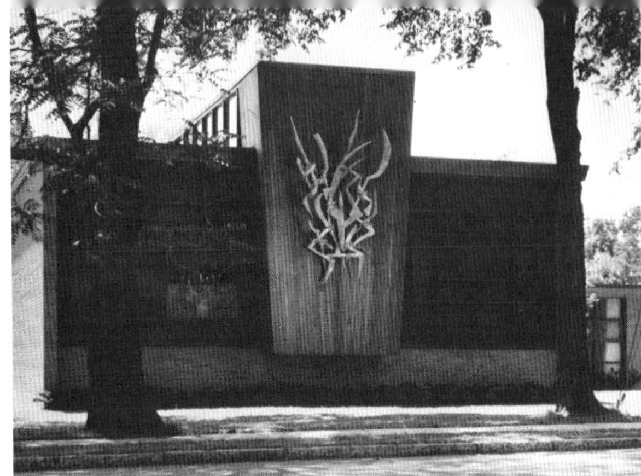

Fig. 24. *". . . and the bush was not consumed,"* 1951.

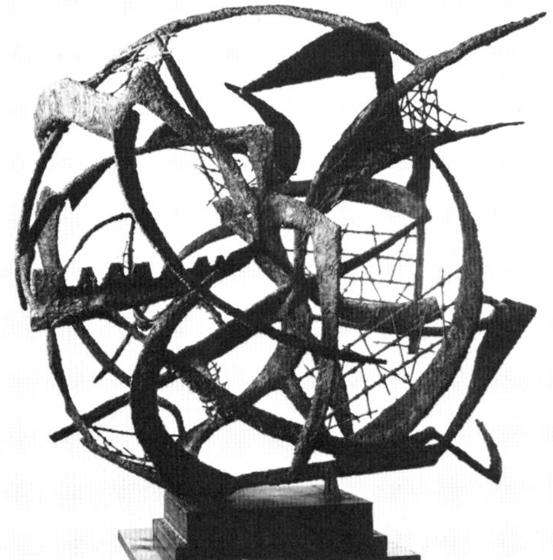

Fig. 25. *Spheroid II*, 1952.

tute, Pittsburgh). This process enriched sculpture greatly by providing an inherent structure for the play of organic shapes, and it held an increasingly important part in the development of Ferber's work after 1949.

Ferber's shift to a more restrained and formal art was prompted in part in 1949-1950 by a rekindled interest in the work of Julio Gonzalez, whom he termed the "father of constructed sculpture."[43] In developing his open sculpture some five years earlier, he first had become aware of and had drawn on Gonzalez, but he was able now to explore and develop new possibilities not previously apparent to him. Gonzalez's example helped free him from Surrealist emotions which by then had begun to run their course and which had come to seem like a rhetorical intrusion between the artist and the work itself. In *Flame* (fig. 20), 1949, the shift became more pronounced as it and subsequent works became vertical and more abstract. They are read as a crisply drawn silhouette, creating a greater feel of light and airy sculpture. "I wanted to get the sculpture up in the air, without actually hanging it there," Ferber later recalled.[44] Here and in *Horned Sculpture* (fig. 21), 1949, and *He Is Not a Man* (fig. 22) of 1950, he enhanced the illusion of lightness by resting the sculptures on a single point. This enabled them to pivot and rotate on the pedestal, which Ferber sought to make as unimportant as possible. These works were considerably larger in both internal scale and physical size, characteristics that also marked the new direction in his sculpture. In addition, they now were composed through a series of disparate parts constituting local and minor accents which we read one by one as they accumulate to form the whole.

The personage theme in *He Is Not a Man* can be traced to the heritage of Miró in whose painting these figures are a constant motif. It recurs in Ferber's sculpture in the fifties as well as in the work of Smith, Lipton, Hare, Roszak, Noguchi, and others at this time. The jagged drawing of the rough biomorphs, here and in *Horned Sculpture,* also corresponds with the broken, scumbled drawing found in contemporary paintings, particularly Clyfford Still's paintings of 1945-1946 and, to a lesser extent, Willem de Kooning's classic pictures *Attic* (Collection The Metropolitan Museum of Art, New York), 1949, and *Excavation* (Collection The Art Institute of Chicago) of 1950. The roughly cut forms at the top of *Horned Sculpture* radically extend the sculpture into space and create a flat, pictorial sculpture which is carried primarily by its drawing and silhouette. These shapes evolved into a more open and fluid, if still spiky and aggressive, drawing in *The Bow* (fig. 23) and in the monumental twelve-foot architectural sculpture of 1951, *". . . and the bush was not consumed"* (fig. 24), commissioned for the façade of the B'nai Israel Synagogue in Millburn, New Jersey. In *Spheroid II* (fig. 25) of 1952, the drawing coalesced into a more pronounced spatial cage which is enclosed by rough outlines[45] containing irregular and broken lines and shapes intertwined in complex movements. The enclosing outlines enabled the piece to become almost freestanding and greatly diminished the presence of the base. In turn, this allowed an even greater freedom of movement of the internal forms in and through space.

Spheroid II was one of Ferber's most successful and important pieces, but he did not pursue immediately the implications of the space-enclosing frame. Rather, his work for

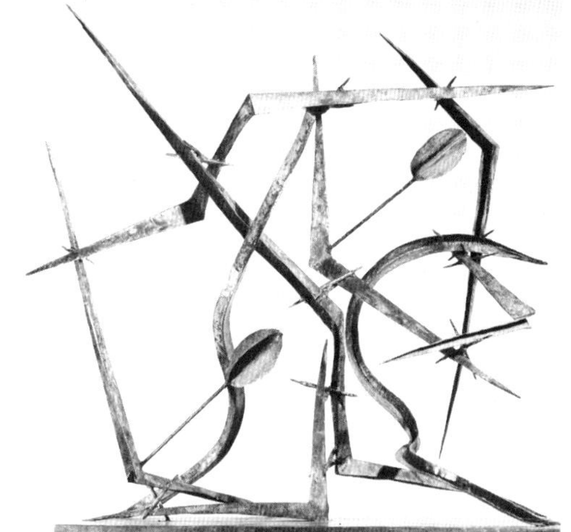
Fig. 26. *Green Sculpture II*, 1954.

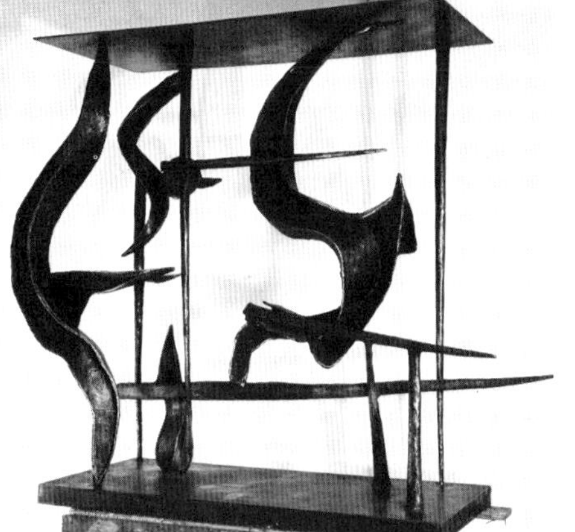
Fig. 27. *Roofed Sculpure with S Curve II*, 1954.

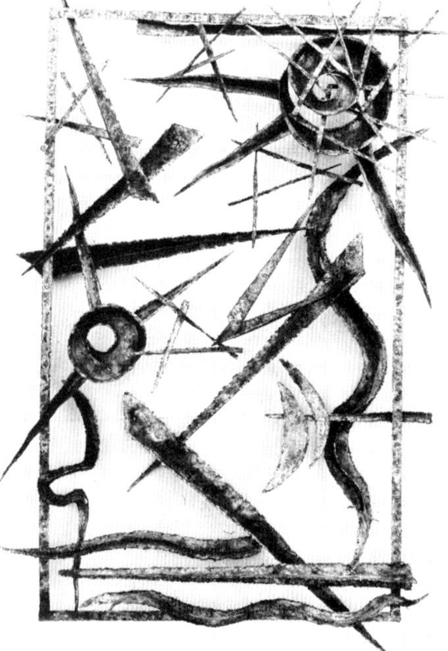
Fig. 28. *Sun, Moon, and Stars II*, 1956.

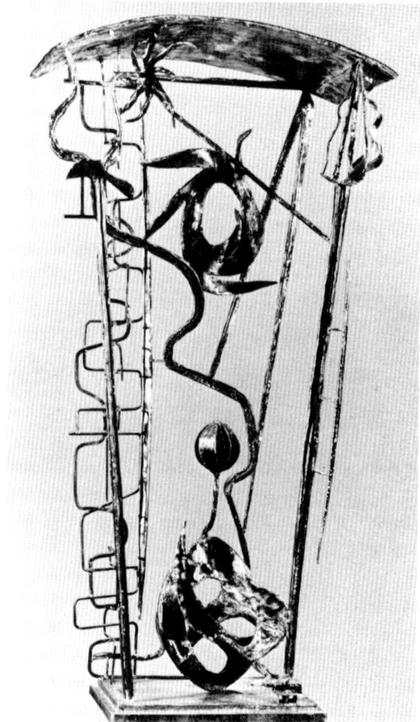
Fig. 29. *Sun Wheel*, 1956.

the next two years followed the direction suggested by the more open, large-scale wall sculpture composed of long, separate, spiky, vertical forms done for the Millburn commission. In *Green Sculpture II* (fig. 26) of 1954, for example, Ferber employed mutations of the abstracted plant imagery first introduced in the Millburn sculpture, now compressed into taut, thin, angular lines which in this context can be read as swords and scythes. This imagery gave Ferber the formal device he needed to "pierce space"[46] through a web of barbed, interwoven lines. The resultant illusion of weightlessness counteracts the traditional mass of sculpture which was identified with an old culture and thus no longer was appropriate to the modern American experience. It is worth noting that the achievement of this illusion has also motivated much of Donald Judd's work,[47] which, of course, stands at opposite poles from Ferber's. Further, John McCoubrey has argued that this characteristic has been at the heart of American art from its inception.[48]

In creating this illusion, however, Ferber came to feel that these sculptures "always seemed to be floating upward, unlimited, or to be sitting at the bottom of a sea of space," as E. C. Goossen phrased it.[49] Ferber also probably was dissatisfied with the extreme attenuation his drawing had reached. He now sought something more solid and substantial within a contained, clearly defined space. At this point Ferber looked back in order to develop and refine the possibilities inherent in the format of the roughly formed space frame in *Spheroid II*. In 1954 in *Roofed Sculpture With S Curve II* (fig. 27), the space frame emerged clearly defined as a strict rectilinear format with a platform base and covering "roof." This format tacitly

acknowledged the framing edges of a painting[50] and appropriated them for the three dimensions of sculpture. The framing roof and platform allowed him to move closer to his goal of "extending forms in space"[51] in a more successful and satisfying way, because the enclosed shapes could touch, move to, and then away from the platform without depending on it for their support. Many of the forms within became bulkier and more solid, consisting of undulating, curvilinear shapes. They are his first use of true calligraphic forms[52] (although the title of a 1953 piece [cat. sculpture checklist #8] had first carried the term), and they contrast with the sharply tapered, menacing spear-like elements. The combination of these contrasting shapes can be traced to Miró's *The Tilled Field*, while the curvilinear elements relate to Kandinsky's painting of the late thirties and to the work of Baziotes and Tomlin of the early fifties. The spear element in turn relates to Giacometti's *Man and Woman* of 1928-1929 (Collection Mme. Henrietta Gomes, Paris). As he has done so often, Ferber absorbed and transformed these diverse sources of painting into a new use in large-scale abstract sculptures.

For the next seven years, Ferber concentrated on exploring and developing an extensive range of structural variations of the space frame. Variants were established in the wall relief *Sun, Moon, and Stars II* (fig. 28) of 1956 and *Sun Wheel* (color plate I and fig. 29) of 1956, which acknowledge and recreate in three dimensions the four framing edges of a painting, two more episodes in Ferber's continuing dialogue between painting and sculpture. The sculptural nature of these formats, however, was established by breaking the edges of the frames in front, in back, and at the sides with the myriad

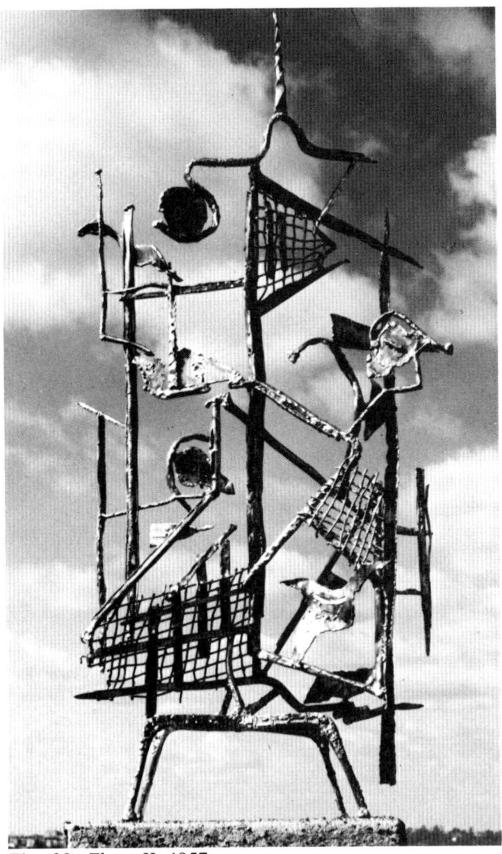

Fig. 30. *Flags II*, 1957.

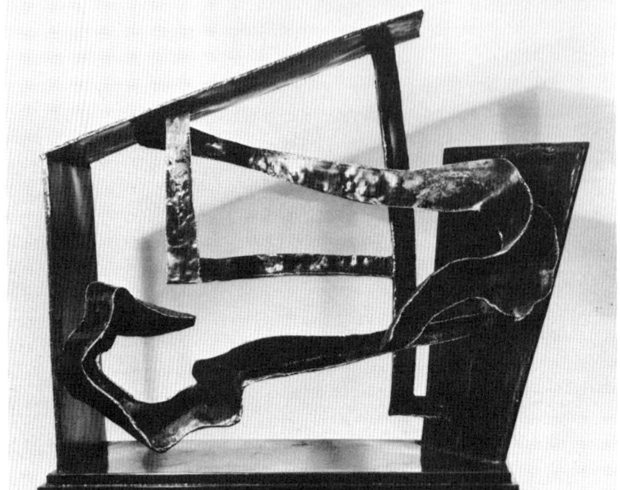

Fig. 31. *Calligraph with Sloping Roof, Two Walls II*, 1957-1963.

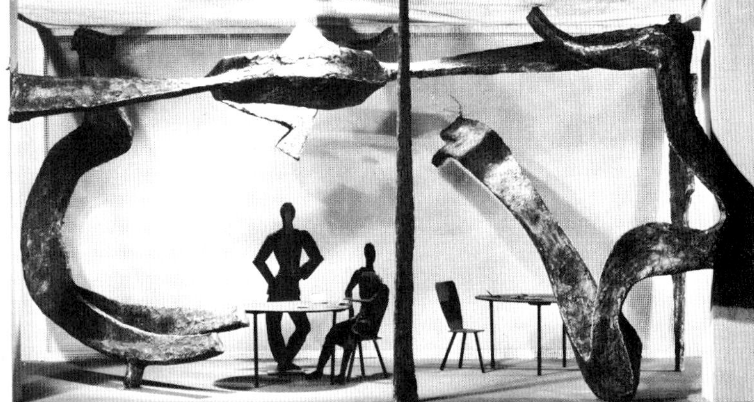

Fig. 32. Model for *Sculpture as Environment*, 1960-1961.

internal shapes. The highly active fields of these works suggest Miró's charged surfaces in *The Tilled Field* and *Harlequin's Carnival* (Collection Albright-Knox Art Gallery, Buffalo) and are in distinct contrast with the more deliberate, slowly moving forms of the roofed sculptures. Artists such as David Smith, Ibram Lassaw, and Richard Lippold, as well as Calder, Peter Grippe, Noguchi, and Seymour Lipton, also had developed personal variations of the space frame by this time. For them it was also an extension of their earlier fusion of the organic and the geometric.[53]

Ferber's *Sun Wheel* elaborated on and opened up the roof and platform first established in *Roofed Sculpture*. It developed a more complex and diverse series of images which unfurl in an easy, relaxed fashion, for it was only in 1956-1957 that Ferber shed the last vestiges of his vocabulary of aggressive, threatening forms. Enhancing the relaxed mood was Ferber's first use of a combination of contrasting materials, here brass, copper, and stainless steel. These varied colors and lustrous surfaces added a new richness and sensuousness that contrasted with the rough, dark surfaces of the earlier work. The lighthearted, almost evanescent, tenor was heightened in *Flags II* (fig. 30), 1957, which invoked an image of banners gaily flowing in the ocean breeze. One is reminded, because of both the imagery and pronounced Cubist grid, of Stuart Davis' scenes of Gloucester Harbor of the mid and late 1930s.

It is worth noting that, in fact, *Flags II* was the only sculpture of Ferber's to engage Cubism directly. In *Flags II*, the four-sided frame of *Sun, Moon, and Stars II* was moved off the wall and set as a flat but three-dimensional sculpture with the enclosing edges broken up in irregular segments. The type of frame and the pictorial quality of the piece created by the forms moving both forward and behind the central plane brings to mind certain of David Smith's works such as *The Letter* (Collection Munson-Williams-Proctor Institute, Utica, New York) of 1950 that investigate the same problems.[54] Each artist, in his own way, used a variant of this format to seek a personal resolution to the common goal of merging the language of painting and sculpture.

Yet another variant of the space frame was proposed by Ferber in *Calligraph with Sloping Roof, Two Walls II* (fig. 31) (begun in 1957 and finished after modification in 1963). Here the calligraphic shapes within are graceful and measured, suggesting a world of harmonious ease, one of "field and harvest," as Robert Goldwater termed it,[55] perhaps stemming in part from the summers he now was spending in Barton, Vermont. The forms are fewer and simpler and unfold lyrically. They do not touch the pedestal and thus mark the first time Ferber was able to eliminate the pedestal as a literal support, a goal he long had sought. The addition of the two side walls to the original format — an addition which may have evolved from the suggestion offered by the four-sided frame of *Sun, Moon, and Stars II* — facilitated this suspension of the formal units in space. The expansion of the roofed sculptures to include side walls, although the roof is tilted and the right wall is splayed at an angle, suggests an enclosed room. The suggestion helped crystallize a train of thought that Ferber slowly and unconsciously had nurtured for some years: the possibility of creating a room-sized environment.

The history of this environment has been well-told by

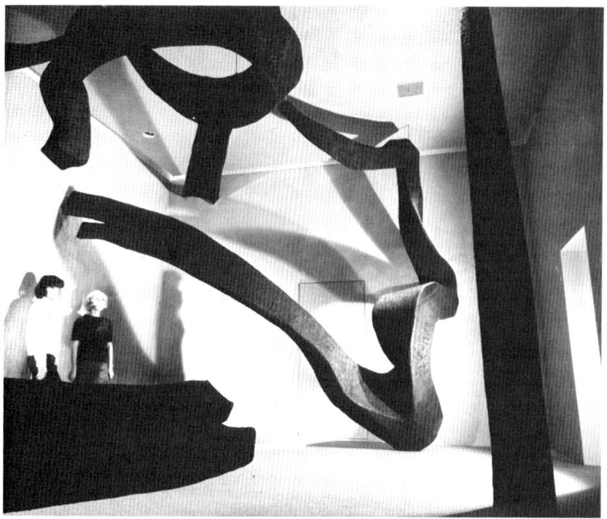
Fig. 33. *Sculpture as Environment*, 1968, as installed at Rutgers University.

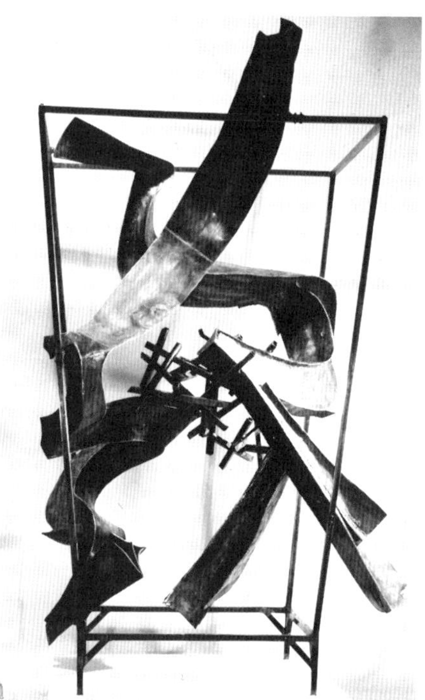
Fig. 34. *Homage to Piranesi IIIc*, 1963.

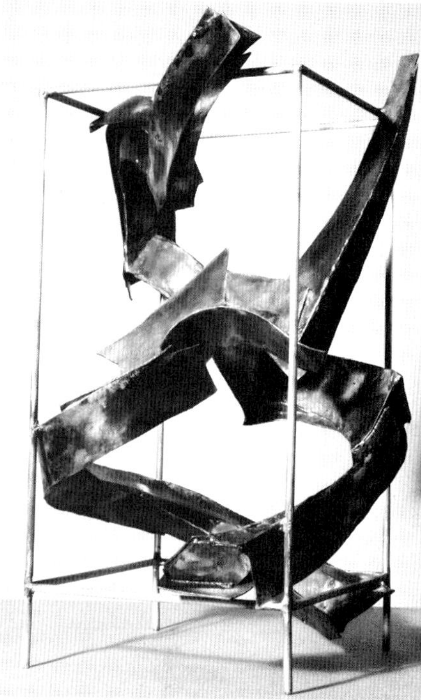
Fig. 35. *Homage to Piranesi V e*, 1965 & 1966.

E. C. Goossen, who was instrumental in its genesis, but it is important to recount.[56] During his trip to Europe in 1938, Ferber had seen Donatello's *Prophets* as they originally were placed, set high off the ground on the façade of the Duomo in Florence. However, on a visit in 1948 he saw them after they had been removed from the façade and were installed at eye level in the Museo dell' Duomo. The effect was dramatic. "There was a depth of form in which one could almost wander and a great intimacy of which there was little indication when they were in place,"[57] Ferber later wrote. In his eyes they had been transformed from a remote image to an intense presence, confirming his belief that one "must engage space physically to experience its symbolic attributes."[58] The impact of that experience was recalled and intensified in 1951 while Ferber was constructing his large Millburn synagogue sculpture, which measured 12 feet, 8 inches high by 7 feet, 10 inches wide by 3 feet deep. Ferber constantly had to crawl in and around it, and he came to feel as if he were actually "in the painting," as Jackson Pollock had referred to the process of making his drip pictures. These events, combined with the development of free-floating forms in the open metal frames from *Spheroid II* to the 1957 *Calligraph with Sloping Roof, Two Walls II,* led during 1958 and 1959 to his focus on the idea of an architectural environment in which one could move freely.

At this time Goossen was in close contact with Ferber, and both felt, and discussed, the need for a type of sculpture that could emulate something of the grandeur and power of large-scale painting, a subject Goossen had dwelled on in his well-known article of 1958, "The Big Canvas."[59] Ferber was devoting a great deal of time to painting in 1958 and 1959,

and he knew firsthand the presence and intimacy of painting he wished to instill in sculpture, one more chapter in his continuing quest to join painting and sculpture. Ferber began experimenting with cardboard to enclose three sides of *Roofed Sculpture with S Curve II* in order to give a sense of what it would be like to "scale down the spectator and permit the work to rise around him and be explored from the inside." Goossen, however, saw that "one could not design something from the outside that was intended to be seen from the inside." As he described it, "I suggested that he build a large box 6 or 8 feet around, with a hole in the bottom to put his head through so that he could view the forms as they developed, simulating somewhat the way they would be seen in the large."[60] The results were far more effective, and Ferber was able to approximate the results he sought. John I. H. Baur, then associate director of the Whitney Museum of American Art, came to see the model and was impressed by it. In November 1960, the museum commissioned Ferber to carry out the environment. It was shown at the Whitney in March-April 1961 as *Sculpture as Environment* (fig. 32), and subsequently in 1968 it was modified slightly and installed permanently at Rutgers University (fig. 33).

The large, broad forms were made of polyvinyl resin and were based on the undulating calligraphs and contrasting verticals developed in the *Roofed Sculptures*. Their effect recalled the architectural fantasies of Piranesi whom Ferber deeply admired, and he incorporated the reference in the titles of his cage sculptures after 1961. The deliberate, almost ponderous unfolding of the calligraphs clearly identified Ferber's sensibility at that time as inalterably baroque. However, the

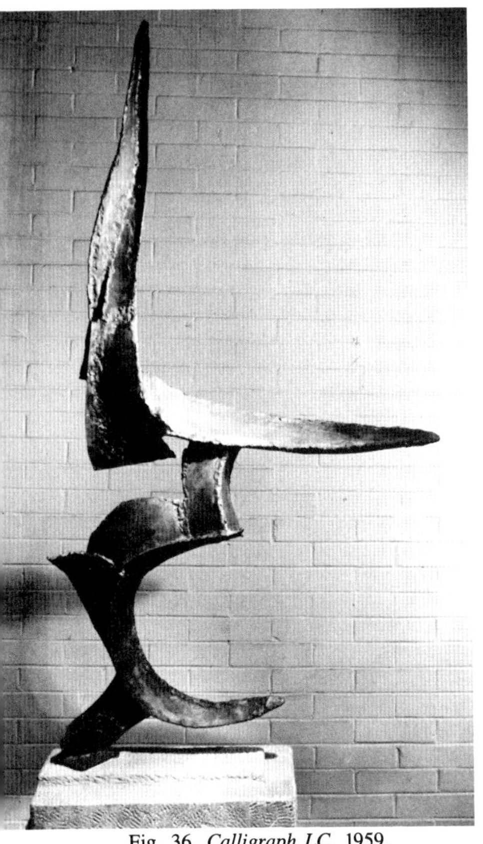

Fig. 36. *Calligraph LC*, 1959.

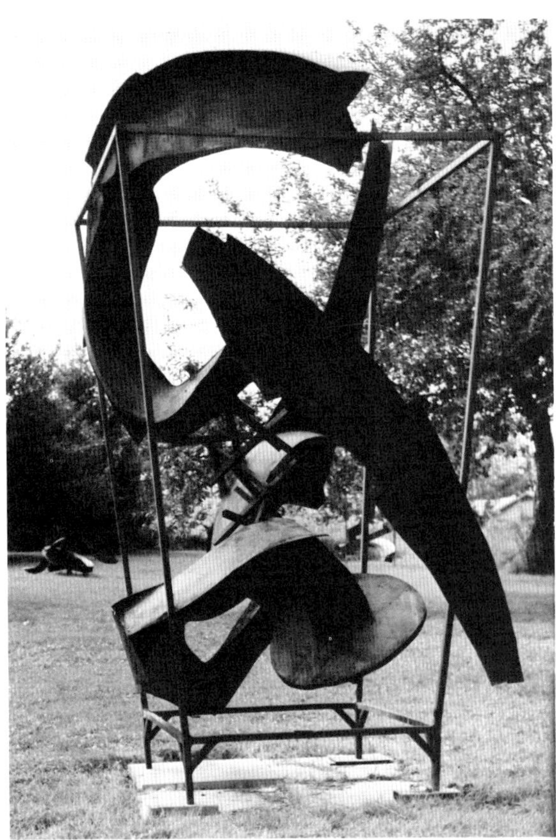

Fig. 37. *Homage to Piranesi IVc*, 1964.

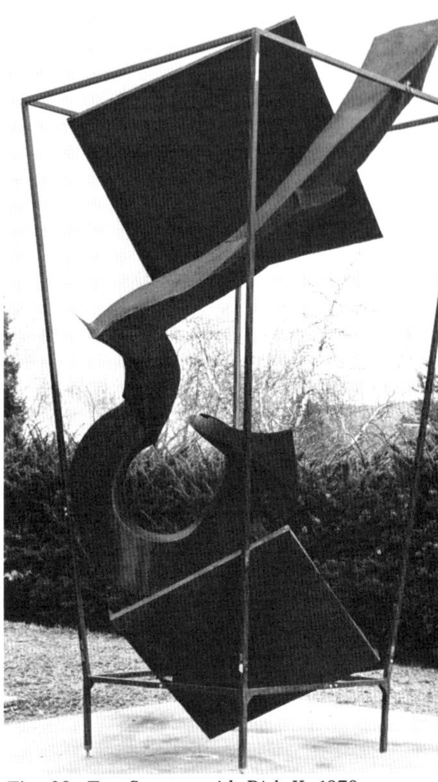

Fig. 38. *Two Squares with Disk II*, 1970.

essence of the Environment is the understanding that the space and one's experience of it were as fundamental to the work as the sculpture itself. As Ferber stated: "I am thinking of a sculpture and a space, each of which would be meaningless if one were to be removed." Ferber was anxious to force the spectator into a "strong, lasting encounter" with the work, one he could avoid only by not entering or leaving the Environment altogether. As such, he saw it as a desirable and necessary alternative to the casual viewing of the usual museum or gallery visitor.[61]

Ferber continued to explore the use of forms suspended in space and the metal space frame, which led in 1961 to his first cage sculptures. These works became his best-known and have provided a format which he has continued to investigate fruitfully to this day. In these sculptures the four walls of the Environment are translated into the four vertical bars of the rectilinear frame, once more implying the framing edges of a painting or drawing paper.[62] The cage frame usually is tapered at the bottom, allowing the internal forms to be suspended more easily and increasing a sense of compression on and within them as they move downward (fig. 34). In some, the bars are set parallel in a way that makes a more equal distribution of weight and mass within the frame more important (fig. 35). His experience with the Environment enabled Ferber to establish successfully a larger scale (most cages are eight to twelve feet high) unprecedented in his freestanding work; in turn, the larger scale created a greater impact and tension through the contrast of the organic forms pushing against and overlapping the bars of the geometric frame. The frame itself was not new, since it was anticipated directly by Giacometti's

similar, although much smaller, structure entitled *Cage* (Collection Modena Museet, Stockholm). But, as William Rubin has pointed out, "The way Ferber used the device — to hold the parts of his sculptures so they could not touch or exert pressure against one another — was new."[63] It is an example of Ferber's ability, as Rubin notes, "to enlarge and reinterpret his experience through working with an established language rather than jettisoning it for a new one."[64]

The cages and, indeed, most of Ferber's work in the late fifties and early sixties are at their best when the calligraph shapes are extended tautly and are held in maximum tension in relation both to the frame and to each other. This effect is achieved most successfully when fewer rather than more forms are used, by avoiding shapes that are too bulky and heavy, and by holding to sharply defined outlines. The same holds true for the sculptures in which the calligraphic shapes were developed individually as vertical freestanding sculptures. The best of these, such as *Calligraph LC* (fig. 36) of 1959, are relatively broad and simple and are read quickly and clearly by the viewer, with no extraneous forms to blur the crispness of the profile. During the sixties, Ferber achieved these characteristics with greater consistency as he became more adept at working within this format. In addition, his work began to reflect certain qualities of post-painterly art, namely the clarity, openness, and directness that marked the work of Kenneth Noland, Frank Stella, Donald Judd, and other artists of the emerging younger generation. In this regard, we often forget that it is important for older artists to let themselves be influenced by younger artists, and it is a sign of Ferber's vitality that he could draw from a new vocab-

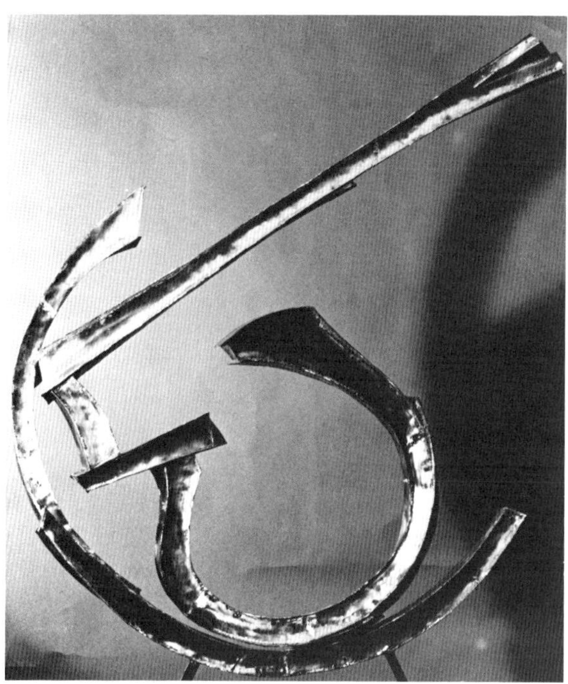

Fig. 39. *Calligraph Sept. 10, '66 III*, 1966.

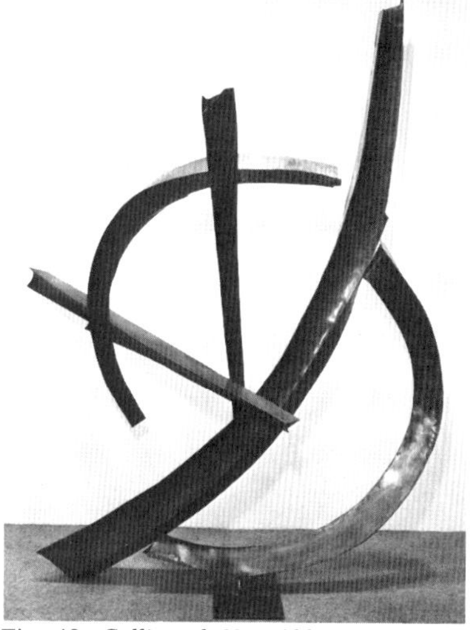

Fig. 40. *Calligraph Nov. '66 III*, 1966-1968.

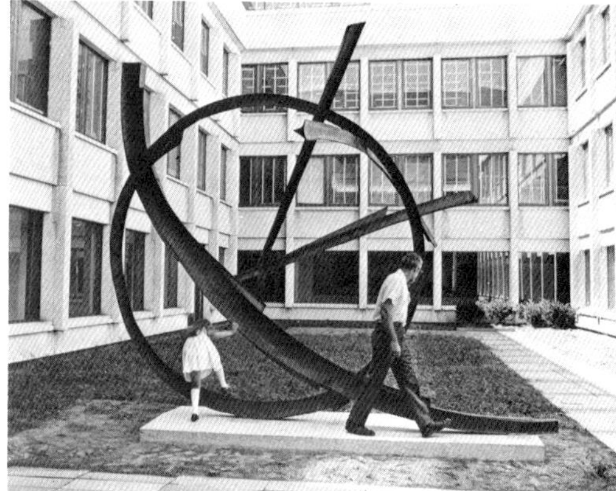

Fig. 41. *Full Circle*, 1966.

ulary and adapt it to his own ends. "I am actively engaged in making art," he has stated, "and I, therefore, am subject to the same forces which affect my younger contemporaries, and what I have to say of the present bears on me, too."[65]

The distinction is clear if we compare *Homage to Piranesi IVc* (fig. 37) of 1964 with a cage of six years later, *Two Squares with Disk II* (fig. 38 and color plate II). Both are powerful and impressive sculptures. But the later piece, with fewer shapes and movements, is tauter and more finely honed, qualities that are heightened by the proportions of the taller and narrower frame. Thus the shapes move in the space with a greater economy and with more directness; the center is kept open, as opposed to the dense cluster of forms in the middle of the earlier cage, giving a sense of greater expansiveness. The line of movement in the 1970 work is fluent and continuous in contrast to the broken, discontinuous lines of the earlier cage. The single, primary thrust of the calligraph in the 1970 cage more sharply delineates the entire work, which we read quickly and easily, thus imbuing the piece with a higher degree of clarity. Even the edges of the shapes are cut more precisely and add to this sense of immediacy. To be sure, the mass and weight of the 1964 cage accumulate in a deeply moving manner, but it does not establish its individual profile with the sureness of the later work. The earlier cage represents the last surge of an older Expressionist language developed in the forties, while the later work looks ahead to new formal possibilities.

In 1966-1968, while working on the cages, Ferber did three

pieces that defined the essence of what was to become a new direction in his work by 1970. The *Calligraph Sept. 10, '66 III* (fig. 39) and *Calligraph Nov. '66 III* (fig. 40) of 1966-1968 are "flat" sculptures, defined by their drawn silhouettes with a new openness and simplicity. They contain an underlying geometry which refers more to the art of the sixties than to the Expressionism of the cages. Ferber in all likelihood could not have taken advantage of this new vocabulary without acknowledging an older type of geometry he first had assimilated in *The Action Is the Pattern* in 1949 and subsequently had developed in the roofed sculptures and the cages. His participation in the structural language of the sixties can be compared with that of David Smith, who was influenced by Kenneth Noland. In 1961-1962, in works such as the polychromed *Circle I, II, and III* (Collection National Gallery of Art), Smith translated Noland's concentric circle paintings of 1960-1961 into the three dimensions of sculpture.[66] Indeed, one can read similar references to Noland's paintings in the half-circle shapes that comprise the enclosing outlines of Ferber's calligraphs of 1966-1968. However, the broken contours of those framing edges must be traced to the circular patterns of the 1952 *Spheroid II*. That the lessons of *Spheroid II* were never far from Ferber's mind at this time is evidenced by the four variations of the work he did after 1952, the last in 1968. However, the feel of the 1966 and 1968 *Calligraphs* is that of the sixties, and an even closer parallel to Noland may be found in the more explicit geometry of *Full Circle* (fig. 41), 1966, a large outdoor piece installed in the John F. Kennedy Office Building in Boston.

In *Ray II* (fig. 42) and *Newport III* (fig. 43), both of

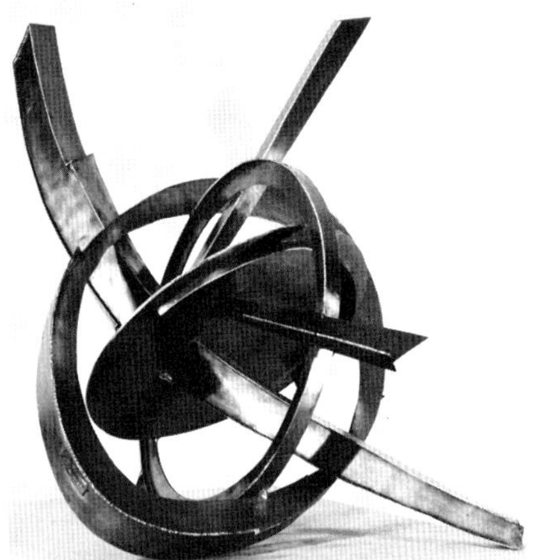

Fig. 42. *Ray II*, 1969.

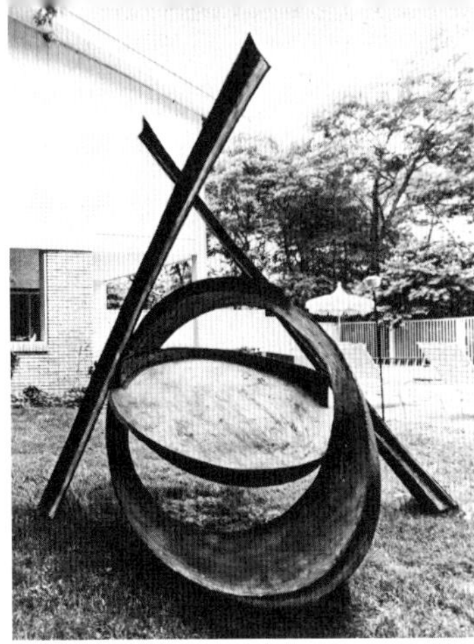

Fig. 44. *Burke II*, 1970.

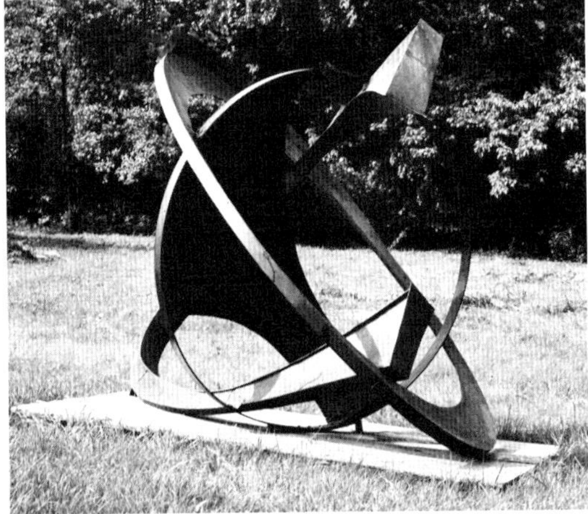

Fig. 43. *Newport III*, 1969.

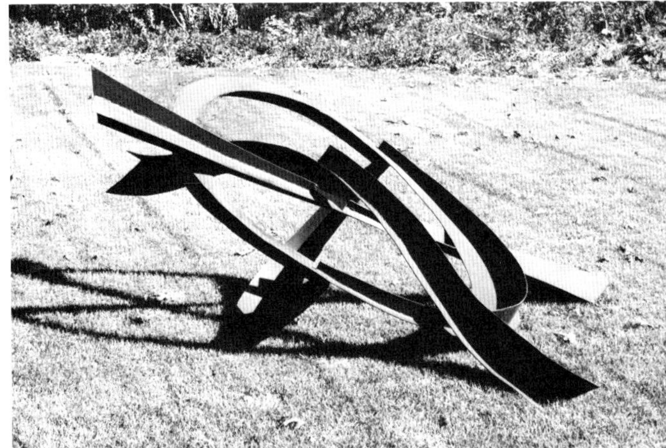

Fig. 45. *Mt. Holly II*, 1970.

1969, Ferber extended the configuration of *Full Circle* into a full three dimensions by joining intersecting segmented circles and ovals in a freestanding structure. The vocabulary now is more planar, geometric, and abstract, imparting a still higher degree of lightness and openness. The intersecting circles of *Newport* are, one might observe, another type of rough sculptural parallel to Noland's concentric circles, but the work more properly must be seen in light of the history of modern sculpture and Ferber's own development of the space frame. Like that of the cage, the format of intersecting circles was, in itself, not new; a precedent can be traced to Rodchenko's *Suspended Composition* of 1920-1921, which Ferber did not know, since it was reconstructed only in 1973 (Collection Museum of Art, Indiana University, Bloomington). It was illustrated in publications such as Moholy-Nagy's *The New Vision* of 1930, but Ferber does not remember seeing reproductions of it. Subsequently the motif was elaborated on by Moholy-Nagy in works such as *Dual Form with Chromium Rods* (Collection The Solomon R. Guggenheim Museum, New York), 1946, by Alexander Calder in his 1934 wire construction *A Universe* (Collection The Museum of Modern Art, New York), and by José de Rivera in works such as *Construction No. 48* (Collection Mr. and Mrs. George Staempfli, New York). What was new was not only Ferber's variation of contour and shape within the circular format but his use of it as a large-scale, freestanding sculpture resting directly on the ground at several points. As such, it constituted a different kind of sculpture than that of the earlier formats. *Newport III* represents another variant of Ferber's circular space frame; it is as if Ferber now wanted to construct a space frame on the

scale of the cages (*Newport* is over seven feet high) but without a literal support. This allowed him to create and define the movement of the internal shapes without using any supporting device except that intrinsic to the forms. Although he realized the importance of the cage format, it appears that Ferber at times had begun to chafe at its constraints.

Segments of intersecting circles and ovals in various configurations thus were established as a basic formal unit of Ferber's new direction. They appear in *Burke II* (fig. 44) of 1970, where they are supported by two flanged poles which crisscross at approximately 45-degree angles; by using only two circular elements, he achieves an even greater simplicity and directness in the work. While flanges of varying height and curvature are welded at right angles to the circles, the shapes themselves are no longer three-dimensional, giving a new degree of lightness and immediacy. These qualities are heightened by the smooth surfaces which now replaced the painterly effects of the rough surfaces in his earlier work. The two supporting poles suggest an informal, "eccentric" variant of the cage structure. However, it is their seemingly informal placement that permits them to assume a more integral structural role than the rectilinear bars of the cages. This was the first of the several variations of the cage that Ferber developed over the next ten years. The placement and vertical thrust of the poles also may be interpreted as an attempt to break out of the confines of the circular space frame of *Newport III* and similar pieces, which Ferber apparently came to view as too restraining.

Ferber was seeking a means to retain the grace and lyricism of the circular motif while opening it up and extending

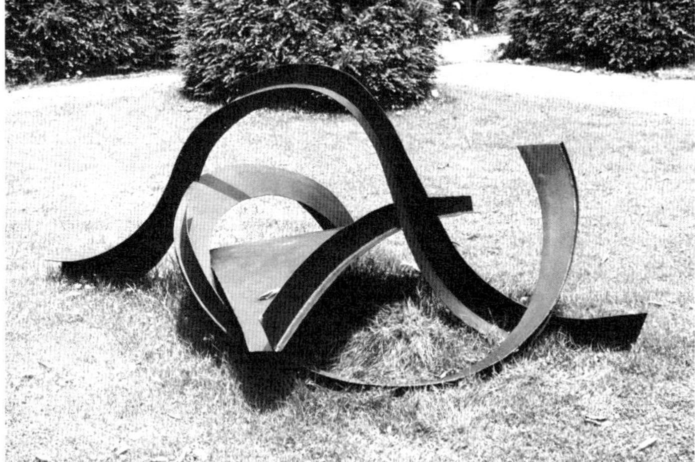

Fig. 46. *St. Johns II*, 1970.

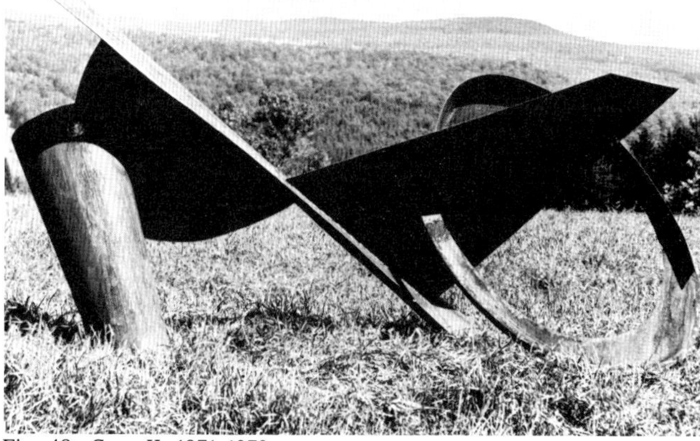

Fig. 48. *Cone II*, 1971-1972.

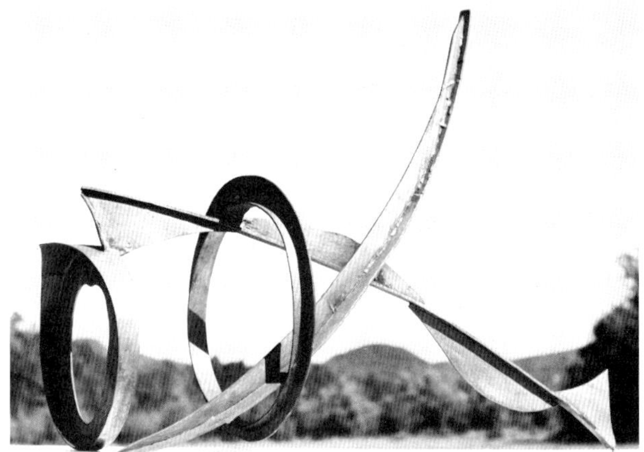

Fig. 47. *Two Rings II*, 1971.

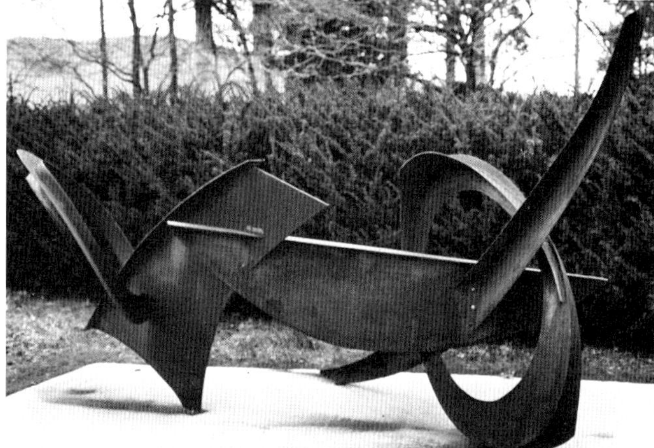

Fig. 49. *Konkapot II*, 1971-1972.

it in a free and cursive manner. In *Mt. Holly II* (fig. 45), 1970, the oval and half-circle were brought low to the ground so that they began to extend horizontally rather than vertically, as they had in *Newport III* and *Burke II*. The horizontal disposition also was made more explicit by the "pole" that cut through the circle to form one support. The appearance here of an undulating arc represented the breaking of a full circle and its reconstitution as a free-flowing linear element. His forms found new freedom to open up when the circular elements were pulled completely apart and extended into flowing shapes in *St. Johns II* (fig. 46), also of 1970. Here Ferber included a roughly triangular element (the first use of this shape) that arched low over the ground.

Ferber's shift to horizontal compositions relates in part to the work of Anthony Caro, who made consistent use of the format in the 1960s. However, and this is an issue he feels strongly about, Ferber had explored horizontal, low-lying sculpture as early as 1946 in *Act of Aggression* as well as *Jackson Pollock* of 1949 and in the *Three Arches II* (fig. 59) of 1964. While he did not pursue the format then, his ability to develop it later no doubt depended on his early experience with it. Moreover, there are major differences between the two artists in their use of it. As William Rubin has noted, Caro's forms are usually simple, anonymous steel construction units that he does not shape before assembling. Thus, "attention is shifted away from them *as forms* in favor of their interrelations, i.e., the syntax of the composition."[67] In Ferber's sculpture, on the other hand, each form is drawn clearly as a strong individual identity. Drawing has remained as important for Ferber in his work of the 1970s and 1980s as it was for

the emergence of his mature style in 1945.[68]

In 1970 and 1971 Ferber introduced a new degree of precision and rigor into shaping forms and structuring his compositions. Each form established a more highly defined profile than the still somewhat tentative outlines in *St. Johns,* and more extensive and complex lateral movements now were introduced. At first the forms and their compositional arrangement were emphatically linear, as in *Two Rings II* (fig. 47) of 1971, and were limited primarily to basic shapes such as the circle and arc. However, in *Cone II* (fig. 48), of 1971-1972, this vocabulary was expanded to include planar shapes such as the cone, the oval, and the triangle. These broader forms allowed a more complex composition and a stronger and more assertive lateral thrust of the shapes. In *Cone II* and *Konkapot II* (fig. 49) of 1971-1972, this thrust gave what Ferber termed a "precarious equilibrium" to the forms.[69] While the elements break back and forth in front and behind the plane established by the horizontal axis, and thus are not completely flat, these sculptures are seen optimally from the front. Ferber did not want to give up the fullness of three dimensions, however, and he continued to develop the cages. In *Homage to Piranesi VII 1 (Oval and Triangle in Cage)* (fig. 50) of 1970-1971, he introduced the same simpler, less painterly elements. He thereby created another range of expressiveness for the cages in which the internal elements were free to develop and unfold in the same way as the freestanding sculptures. Indeed, these cages took on the same openness and lightness, qualities made all the more intense by the sensuous effects of color and surface created by contrasting the bright brass frame with the dark Cor-Ten steel.

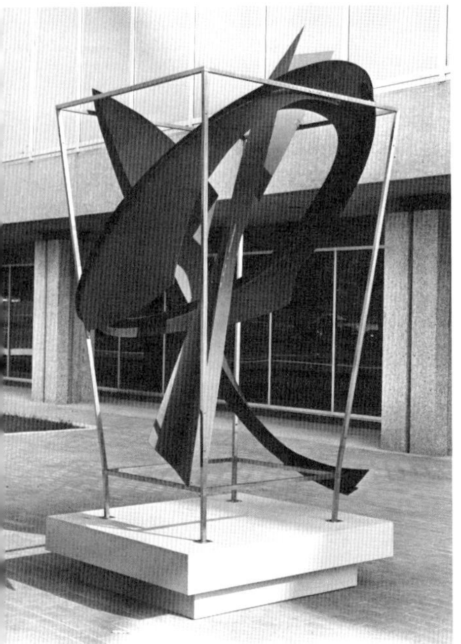

Fig. 50. *Homage to Piranesi VII 1*
(Oval and Triangle in Cage), 1970-1971.

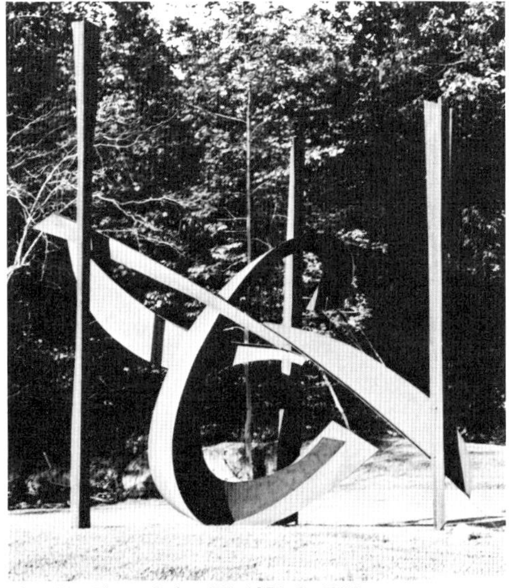

Fig. 51. *Three Poles III*, 1971 & 1975.

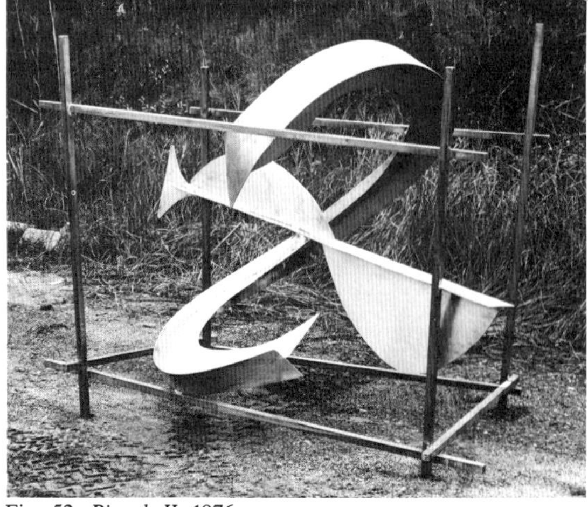

Fig. 52. *Pisgah II*, 1976.

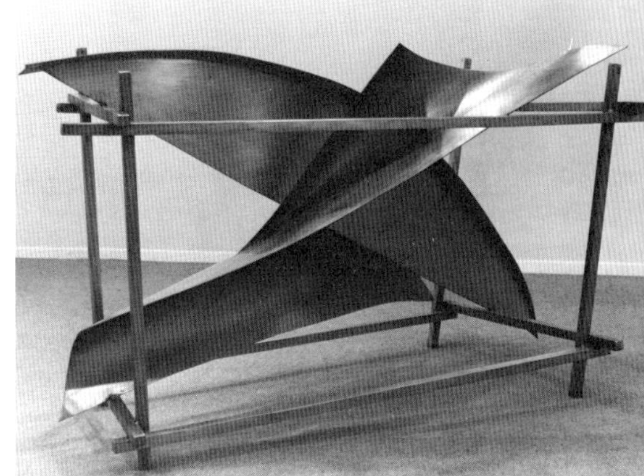

Fig. 53. *Cleft II*, 1977-1978.

One might conclude that working with the literal supports of the cage served one side of his artistic persona, while his engagement with the more informal lateral sculptures served another. In fact, his art has evolved around these two poles since 1970. The distinctions, however, are far from absolute, and one enriches the other, one is simultaneously nourished and tempered by the other. That is, the horizontal works seem to need a governing internal rigor to give them maximum extension and impact. The cages, on the other hand, seem to need the freedom of invention permitted by the new vocabulary in order to continue to renew themselves formally. This interdependence and cross-fertilization is another aspect of the old fusion of the geometric and the organic that has been central to Ferber and to advanced American sculpture since 1930.

The subsequent reinvigoration of the cages led to still other variants of the format, thus extending once more the formal and thematic range of Ferber's work. We already have noted the first such variant in *Burke II,* in which the poles were liberated from the confines of the frame. This allowed Ferber to enlarge and incorporate them as freestanding elements which also support the interior shapes in *Three Poles III* (color plate IV and fig. 51) of 1971 and 1975, the largest independent piece Ferber had done to date. The interior shapes are a segmented circle and two sweeping, flanged arcs of reverse curves, elements which remained basic to his work even as the range of shapes was expanded and diversified during the seventies. *Pisgah II* (fig. 52) begun in 1970, but modified and finished in 1976, and *Cleft II* (fig. 53), 1977-1978, introduced a low, horizontal variant of the cage. Here, the informal structure of the frame was submitted to its own process of loosen-

ing up that was in keeping with the spirit of the new direction his work had taken. The bars are of unequal height and are no longer strictly parallel. They seem almost as if they could shift and slide, as if their positioning could be adjusted, thus implying a potential movement. As a result, the frame appears to be more closely a part of the internal forms, in contrast to the distinction between frame and internal form that was strictly maintained in the original cages. A formal role even is reversed in the lateral variation of the cage, because the horizontal element that cuts diagonally through it is more rigid and strictly "geometric" than the bars in the frame, just the reverse of the relationship between internal forms and the frame in the cages. Such formal plays and relationships account for the richness of Ferber's work. "Geometric" is used advisedly in considering Ferber's post-1968 work; it is not absolute but relative geometry, compared with that, for example, of Minimal art. Ferber always insists on retaining a handmade look; edges are always a little rough, and ovals, arcs, and circles are never perfect, but are, rather, approximate.

Ferber reached a pinnacle of accomplishment in the monumental *Egremont II,* (fig. 54 and color plate III), completed in 1972 and installed the next year on the grounds of the Pasadena Museum of Modern Art. He expanded his basic vocabulary of the circle, oval, triangle, and flanged shafts to include a small and a much larger planar pylon, one in the form of a truncated triangle and the other a trapezoid. These new elements allowed new types of compositional accents to be introduced to the work. The large pylon at left, for example, both initiates and contains and deflects movement within the piece. The two "poles" which cross and overlap at roughly

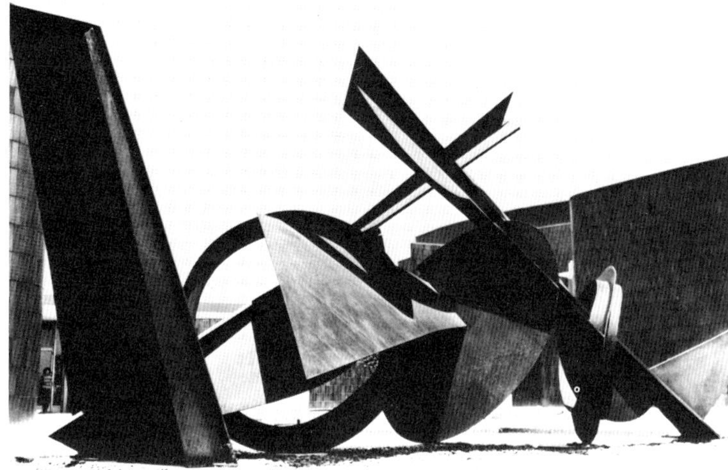

Fig. 54. *Egremont II*, 1971-1972.

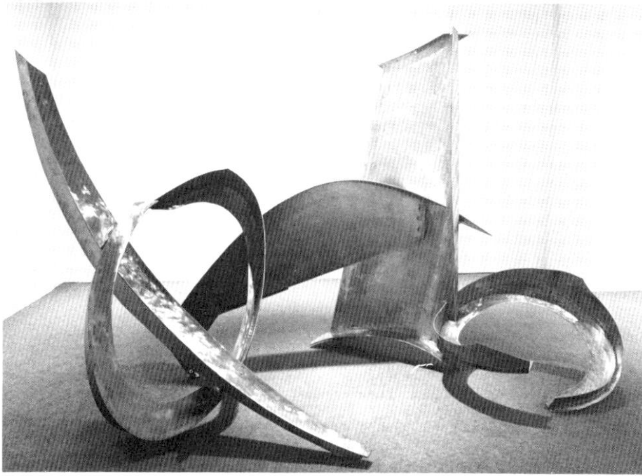

Fig. 56. *Lenox II*, 1975.

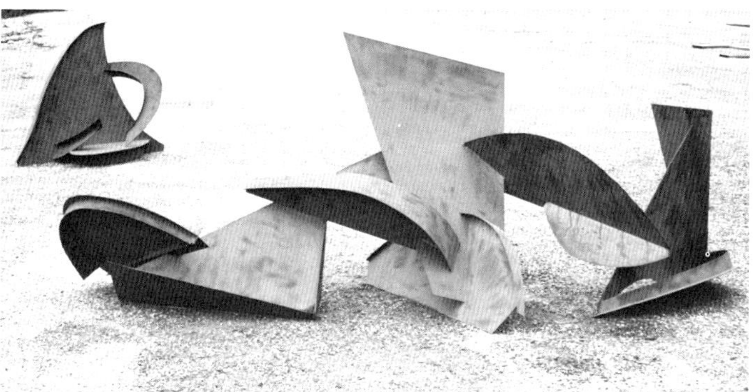

Fig. 55. *MacDougal III*, 1972-1974.

the center hover over and support two circles, an oval, and a triangle which are suspended from them in a way that first was developed in *Burke II*. Here, it is made far more complex and subtle and is incorporated as part of a composition that achieves a masterful cadence of pacing, of movement and repose, of balance between curve and straight edge, plane and void. *Egremont II* unfurls itself through a system of rhythmic and contrapuntal accents that calls to mind the spatial divisions in Picasso's small 1938 *Bathers on the Beach* (Zervos VII, 216; Collection Musée Picasso), although the relation no doubt is fortuitous. In each, as we read the composition laterally, verticals play against triangles, and in turn they are touched by circular shapes and are pulled along by diagonal thrusts, with individual shapes and areas interrelated yet standing independent as they unfold. Ferber referred to this kind of movement in describing *Egremont II* and other sculptures of the period when he described their forms as

touching, penetrating, encircling in a kind of silent and unmoveable choreography. . . . These "horizon" sculptures are extended like a frieze — the choreographic reference is to the kind of tensions set up in a group of dancers as they move in relation to each other. Emotional and psychological tension is produced when the forms seem to move. . . . These tensions are a metaphor for our own.[70]

Ferber's reference to "horizon" sculptures is worth noting. Many of his works of the 1970s have been named after towns and sites in the Berkshires near North Egremont, Massachusetts, where he has spent long summers since 1972. Prior to that he had summered for many years in Barton, Vermont. It is tempting — and not difficult — to equate the low-rolling hills of the New England landscape that are so much a part of his life with the undulating movement of the arcs in works such as *MacDougal III* (fig. 55) of 1972-1974. One could not call Ferber's work "landscape" sculpture in the sense of David Smith's *Hudson River Landscape*, 1951 (Collection Whitney Museum of American Art, New York) or David Hare's *Sunset* (Collection The Museum of Modern Art, New York) of 1953, which are based on literal landscape images. Rather, the mood, the poetic and lyrical movement of such pieces can recall the gentle, natural forms of the Berkshires.

The course of Ferber's mature art has been toward broader, simpler forms, and the work of the 1970s was no exception. However, by no means has it followed a straight line. (Ferber had said earlier that he did not work in one set direction — that he "moved forward, then back to an earlier idea and then forward again, as the sparrow goes."[71]) Thus, from the relative complexity of *Egremont II* and *MacDougal III*, Ferber returned to a simpler format in *Lenox II* (fig. 56 and color plate VI) of 1975, one of his best works. Its success is due in large part to the full articulation of each element (the configuration is a refinement and modification of *Konkapot II*). Each is read as a separate part, and its contact with the other elements is kept to a minimum. The forms also impress themselves on us so clearly because the luster of the polished brass gives this work, more than any other in his oeuvre, an almost optical quality when viewed under strong light. While Ferber has been struck by the compelling surface of brass, he has been wary of the possible dissolution of the forms that might result from these optical effects. Therefore, he has not

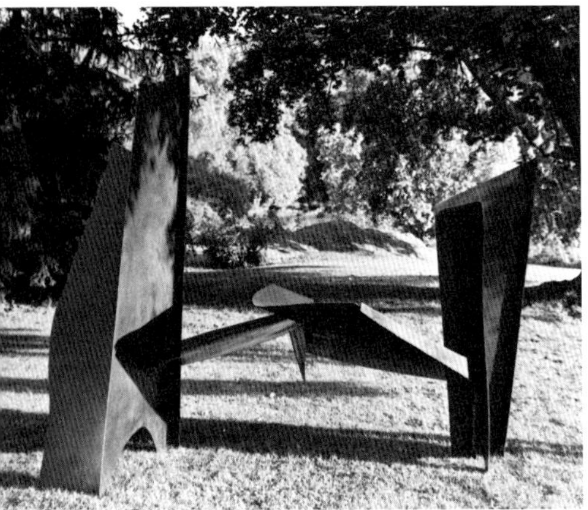

Fig. 57. *Williams IIIa*, 1976.

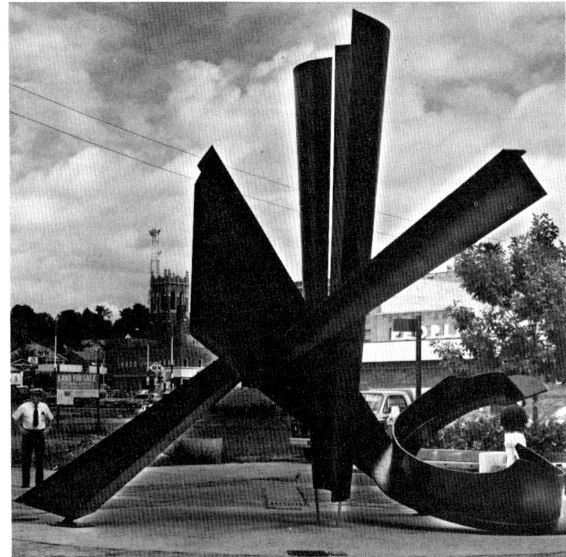

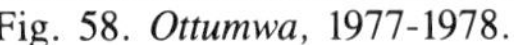

Fig. 58. *Ottumwa*, 1977-1978.

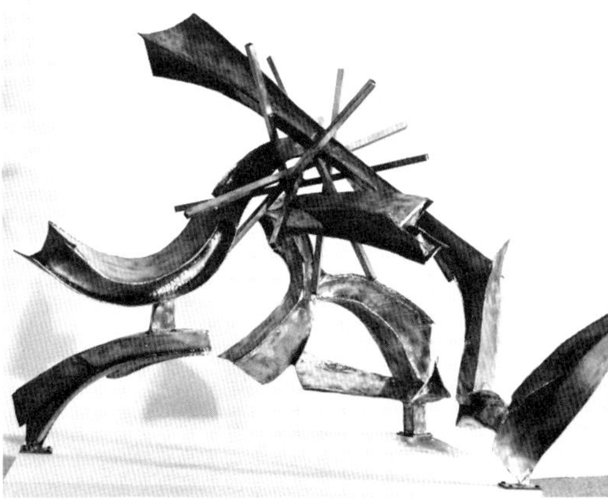

Fig. 59. *Three Arches II*, 1964.

pursued its use,[72] except with a relatively dull finish in pieces such as *Pisgah II* and in combination with other materials.

Lenox II was the last work to employ the basic set of "regular" geometric shapes that had informed the sculpture from 1970-1975. Ferber may have been at pains to ensure that his work did not become locked into a set pattern, that its format did not become too predictable or confining. Along with a shift to simpler forms, Ferber also reduced the number of elements in a given piece. In addition, he introduced shapes that, while retaining their source in a type of loose geometry, are modified by the artist and become more irregular and unpredictable. In the *Williams* (fig. 57 and color plate VII) series of 1976-1977, for example, the two supporting pylons are not new to his work. However, their shapes are made more complex by the freely drawn flanges that are welded to the back of them at right angles, with the larger one opened up by the elongated oval cut out at the bottom. In turn, the pylons are set at right angles to each other. Within this strict outline, the internal oval shapes are compressed tightly, and they break and intersect with each other at sharp and unexpected angles. The vertical supports, which now relieve the horizontality of the earlier works, might be compared with those in Caro's work of 1972-1973 such as *Veduggio Flat* (Collection Guido Goldman Sprinkling Trust, Cambridge, Massachusetts). In such works Caro introduced his own irregular drawing and pulled back from the rigor of his earlier work. However, the central element in Caro's work is larger and more prominent and is also lower to the floor while running parallel to it. The supports themselves are linear and purely invented, while those in Ferber's piece have an approximate

geometric basis. Furthermore, the format of the vertical supports joined by arching forms has its own history in Ferber's work, since it can be traced to *Jackson Pollock* of 1949.

In 1977 Ferber was commissioned by the City of Ottumwa, Iowa, to do a large sculpture for a new pedestrian mall in the old center of town, which was in the process of renewal. It was completed and installed in 1978. *Ottumwa* (fig. 58), standing eighteen feet high and twenty-two feet wide, is arguably Ferber's best and most beautiful work. It culminated his long involvement with public art, an area in which he holds an important and pioneering place. He had been trained in architectural sculpture, and his first effort in this direction began as early as 1946 when he submitted a proposal to the competition for the Kleinhaus Music Hall in Buffalo. Public commissions offered him the chance to work on a large scale, an important aspect of Ferber's work since it relied as much on space as on mass, and the space was articulated more fully when the scale was larger. As a practical matter, Ferber only could do large pieces in a place set aside especially for them. However, his involvement with public art also has been motivated by a genuine concern for the relation of the modern artist to society. In the 1940s he saw an inevitable and even necessary schism between the artist and the public, but over the years he has come to feel that this distance has closed considerably.[73] He long has urged that sculptors, painters, and architects work together to achieve a common good, namely the extension of man's experience, but these pleas usually have fallen on deaf ears.[74]

Ferber's commission (Gottlieb and Motherwell also re-

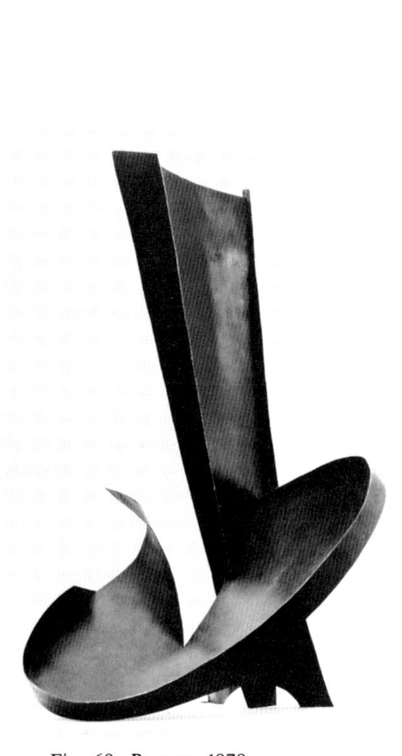

Fig. 60. *Roanne*, 1978.

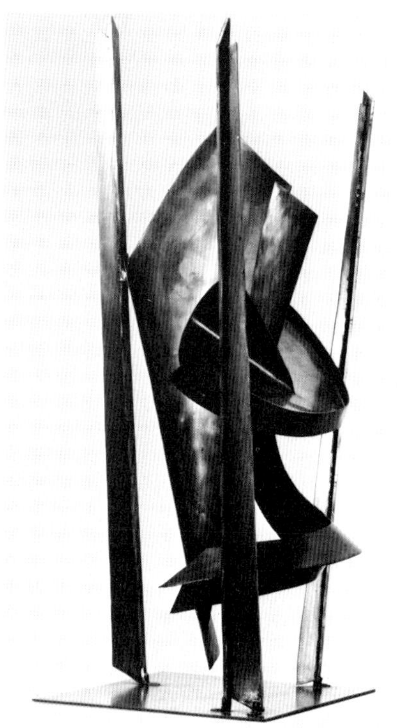

Fig. 61. *Velay*, 1978.

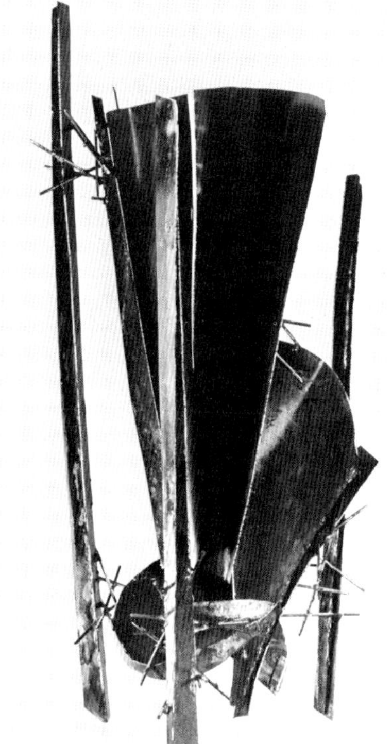

Fig. 62. *Baldwin Hill*, 1979.

ceived commissions) for the B'nai Israel Synagogue in Mill-burn, New Jersey, in 1951, was his first, and it engaged his full attention for an entire year. Ferber remembers that the commission was the subject of some controversy among his circle of artist friends. Newman urged him to carry it out, since it would put the new art squarely in the public's eye. Ad Reinhardt, on the other hand, opposed the commission on the grounds that it was antithetical to the private, introspective nature of the group's art.[75] Thereafter Ferber carried out commissions for the Temple Aaron in St. Paul, Minnesota, and Temple Anshe Chesed in Cleveland in 1956, both of which were wall reliefs related to *Sun, Moon, and Stars II* of the same year. In addition to the *Sculpture as Environment,* Ferber also developed *Three Arches* of 1962-1963 as a proposal for an environment in an outdoor setting in Vermont. Although the original plan was never executed, it did result in two smaller, freestanding versions of the piece (fig. 59) and a fifteen-foot version now at Rutgers University. The sculpture for the Kennedy Office Building in Boston (1966) and *Egremont II* (although not strictly a public commission) also should be considered as part of this history.

Ottumwa is a formal triumph in its own right, but much of its success stems from how well it functions in its site, which is not always the case with public sculpture. In keeping with his willingness to shift direction, to move back in order to explore older ideas anew, Ferber reintroduced a verticality that anchors the sculpture to the site and establishes it as a beacon for the space the sculpture defines. At the same time, the verticality is modified by the spread of the supporting diagonal and the segmented circle. This makes the diameter larger than the height, enabling us to understand the work as laterally expanding simultaneously with the vertical thrust. Relatively few and simple elements are used, but they are articulated so carefully that myriad — and surprising — views unfold as we move around it. The vertical element is formed by two reversed half-cones, a device which keeps our eye shifting from one side of the piece to another. The cone had appeared first in the work, titled *Cone II*, done in 1971-1972. However, only in *Ottumwa* and subsequent works did Ferber develop the motif as a fertile addition to his sculptural language. The reversed curves of the cones are contrasted in turn by the segmented circle which forms a supporting element and which moves up into space, leading us to its point of intersection with one of the two diagonals. These familiar diagonal elements are far wider than before and now call to mind I-beams that have been sliced at irregular angles. But so that we do not associate the configuration of an I-beam with implied weight, Ferber curls the under-edge of the larger diagonal. This light, elegant touch in turn echoes and enters into a subtle dialogue with the curves of the circle and the vertical half-cones. Such elements give evidence that not the least of the successes of *Ottumwa* is the integration of local nuance and accent within the context of a large-scale sculpture of considerable power and impact. So, too, this touch is another example of the fusion of the geometric and the organic, now refined to the point where the fusion occurs *within and as part of the same element*. Thus, the central vertical element is both a vigorous geometric thrust into space and a gentle undulating line. The second of the crisscrossing diagonals is now two separate elements seemingly cut in half and then turned

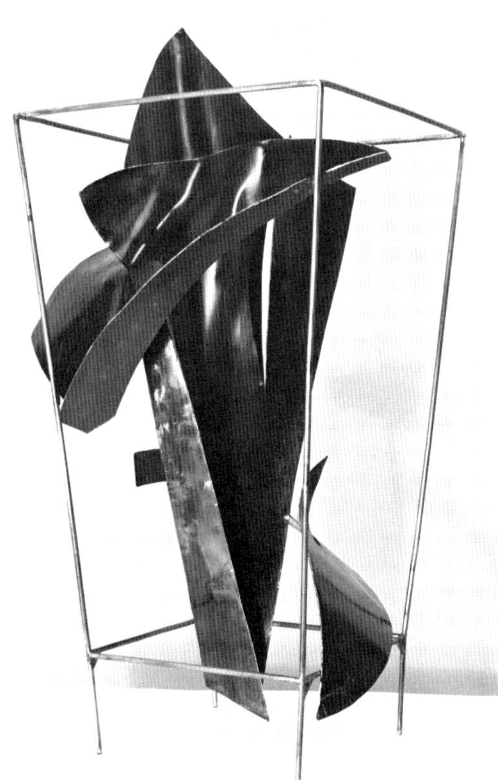

Fig. 63. *Homage to Piranesi X (Sens)*, 1978.

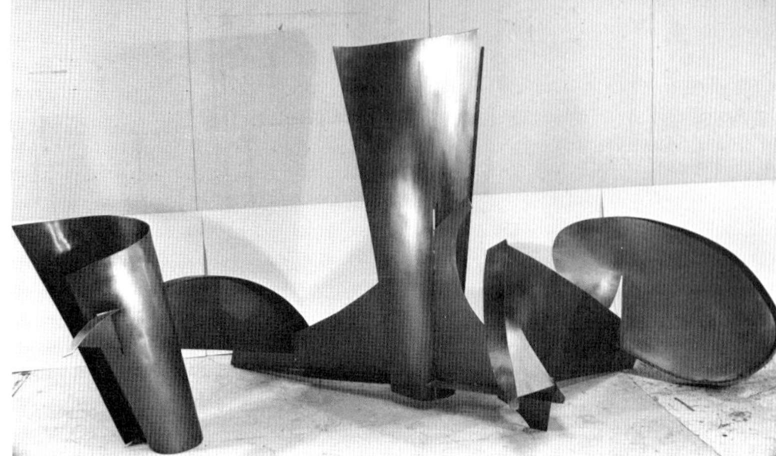

Fig. 64. *Canaan II*, 1977-1978.

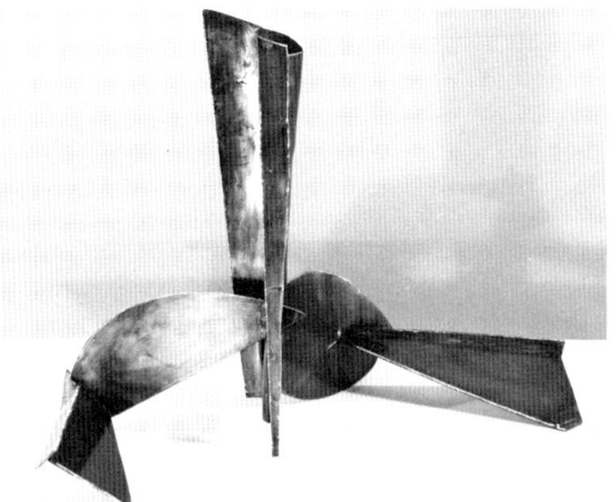

Fig. 65. *Bleeker*, 1978.

over and repositioned at a different angle to the other support. Thus, just enough of a discordant note is introduced to jar the piece gently off balance, keeping it from becoming too settled. This internal movement acts as a pivot for the work which seems to turn on its site, giving a new, always changing definition and focus to the axes of the malls.

The sculpture is as rich, as lyrical and poetic, as the rolling and fertile hills of the southeastern Iowa farmland in which Ottumwa is located. Its formal workings and mechanics are appropriate to a town situated in an area filled with and dependent on arsenals of complex and powerful farm equipment. The sculpture thus seems at ease in its surroundings as almost an indigenous part of the town and the land. It also is appropriate because it relates easily and naturally to Ottumwa's other public sculptures from earlier eras closely tied to the town's history; a monument to Civil War veterans and another to the Indians of the region bespeak the experience and values of another time just as Ferber's bespeaks those of modern America.

The vertical emphasis of *Ottumwa* continued in *Roanne* (fig. 60) and *Velay* (fig. 61), both of 1978, and in *Baldwin Hill* (fig. 62) of 1979. In the latter two works, variants of the open cone are used as the primary interior element and are supported by three poles that mark yet another adaptation of the cage. The open vertical cone also appears as the dominant, central shape in the cage sculpture *Homage to Piranesi X (Sens)* (fig. 63), 1978, giving the original cage format still another expressive inflection. The open cone used as the central motif in *Ottumwa* also appeared in *Canaan II* (fig. 64) of 1977-1978 both as the primary vertical element at center and

as a smaller form comprising contrasting curves at the left, permitting a careful equilibrium between vertical thrust and lateral projection. In *Bleeker* (fig. 65), 1978, the single vertical conical element is flanked by low-lying and arching half ovals. These works approach a state of art as abstract as music. Ferber has said of these works that he often gets a general idea for a sculpture while at a concert.[76] Ferber can move in and out of his work with such ease and assurance, shifting here, modifying there, that in *Baldwin Hill* he could reintroduce the clusters of barbed spikes that had been a distinguishing characteristic of his Surrealist work of the late forties. In turn, he had developed the clusters from examples he had found in the earlier Giacometti, Gonzalez, and African fetish figures. The clusters also appeared in *Four Poles*, 1979 (fig. 66), where another form of the space frame was engendered by the cross between the larger, freestanding elements of *Three Poles III* of 1971 and the "lateral" cage structure of *Pisgah II* and *Cleft II;* here, the poles support the internal shapes so they have no need to touch each other, allowing them to suspend themselves even more fully and freely in space.

The sculpture done in steel after 1976 generally has been painted with a marine varnish mixed with black tinting color, giving a rich, lustrous surface. This mixture had solved the problem of the rough surfaces of Cor-Ten steel, which sometimes seemed too heavy. In addition, it does not have the feeling of a color that has been applied arbitrarily. The mixture catches light, but it is not highly reflective and does not create an optical quality, and it seems intrinsic to the material. This is the first consistent success Ferber has had with painting his surfaces. He had painted a version of the 1954 roofed sculpture

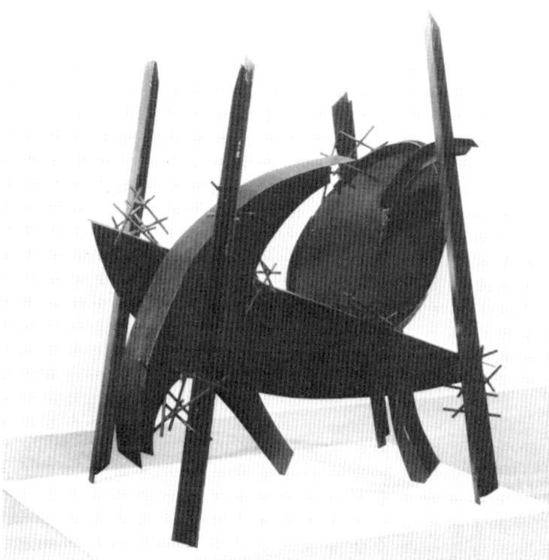
Fig. 66. *Four Poles*, 1979.

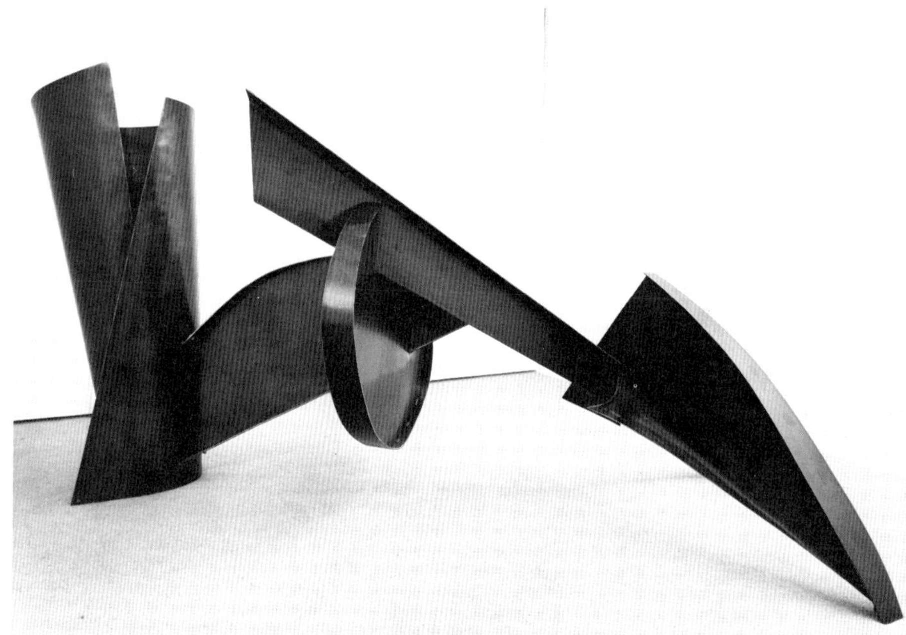
Fig. 67. *Notch View*, 1978.

(now destroyed) yellow, but he felt it added nothing formally. He used it again for only one work in 1966 and then again in the early seventies when he applied a thin purple coat to a few pieces. These last uses also seemed arbitrary, however, and Ferber since has restored the original surfaces.

The unwinding, open-ended syntax, now interspersed with drawn and invented shapes, coexists easily with the more formal works of the cage series and its variants. In *Notch View* (fig. 67 and cover) of 1978, for example, the familiar cone, with a circle and half-oval, are hooked together and sent sweeping through space by the large bending arrow, one of the most singular and compelling shapes in the entirety of Ferber's sculpture and indeed in all of recent sculpture. The element reminds us of Miró and the late work of Kandinsky in the sheer exuberance and power of the drawing. The shaping and drawing in parts of *Chesterwood* (fig. 68) of 1979 hark back to Ferber's early calligraphy and even hint at the Baroque turnings found in the early cages, not with the weight and bulk of those works, but with an offhand, meandering line and movement. These sculptures contrast with a new series of wall reliefs of 1979 and 1980 (figs. 69, 70) which recalls the format of the 1956 relief *Sun, Moon, and Stars II,* although the frame's geometry is now made in a more relaxed format. The frame is bent to the formal needs of the cut internal shapes that again move in front of and behind the frame. They are one more example of Ferber's gift for reinvigorating an old format with new possibilities.

If Ferber has been engaged in easy discourse with his sculpture,

he has, at the same time, increasingly become impatient with it. In the last four years he has done very little sculpture and has devoted most of his time to painting, which he now sees as a new and more powerful challenge.[77] This recent painting campaign began in 1973, the first having extended from 1958 to 1963. But it is true that, as Ferber insists, he never really has stopped painting. He began early as a painter and etcher and stopped exhibiting his paintings regularly only after 1935. As we have seen, his sculpture has depended for its inception on his constant drawing, and many of these drawings are, in fact, small paintings. Taken together, these drawings establish a greater continuity to his painting than publicly has been visible. The first large-scale paintings that appeared in 1973, for example, depended on a series of small paintings on paper which he had done in 1970-1972.

Ferber's impatience with sculpture can be traced to 1948 in a statement he wrote for the magazine *Tiger's Eye.* Ferber noted the problem that sculpture faces because it has an "existence in a prosaic sense," that it is "another object like a bottle or table." This, he said, "makes painting easier to confront. . . . Looking at painting, one escapes the fact of mass." For Ferber, then, sculpture was "difficult to grasp as fantasy and image," an objection which he still holds. "Painting is a direct communion," he wrote, and he values this immediacy above all else in painting.[78] In the late forties, Ferber had few friends among the sculptors who, he felt, spent far too much time talking about techniques and materials. He preferred the company of the painters who seemed more disposed to speak of ideas and the actual making of art. This predilection would ensure that painting was never far from his mind, especially with a

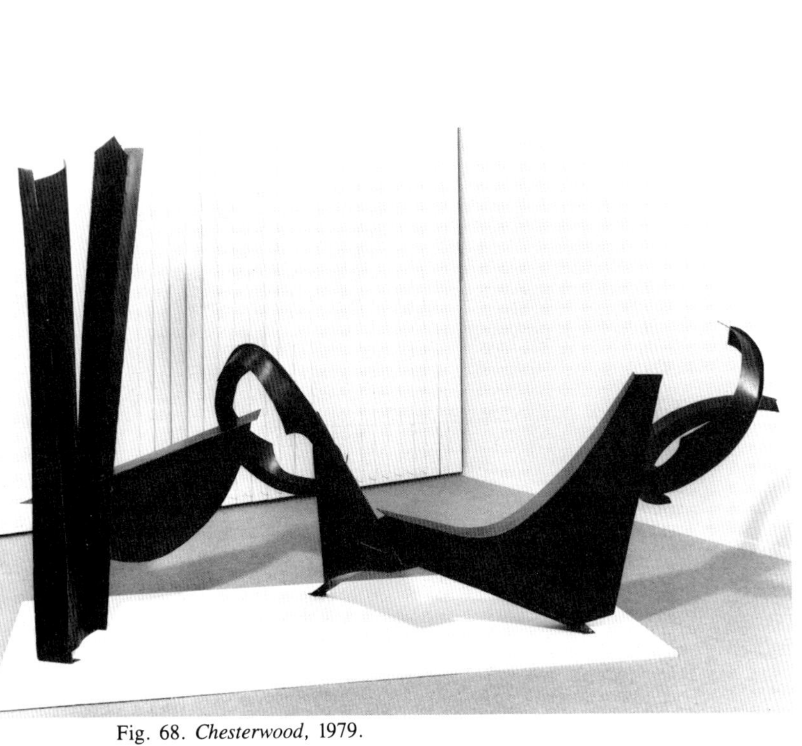

Fig. 68. *Chesterwood*, 1979.

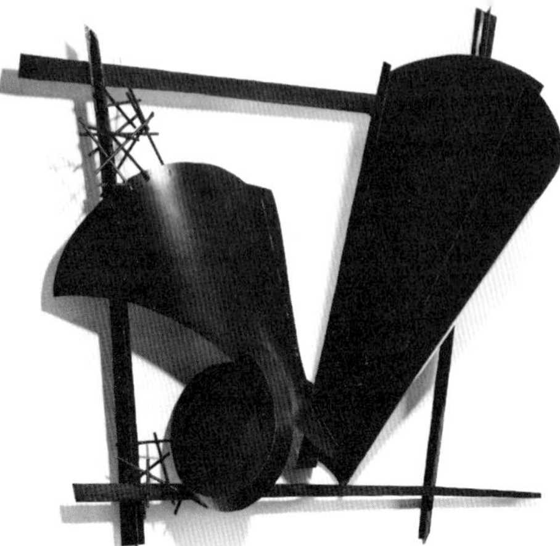

Fig. 69. *Wall Sculpture I*, 1979.

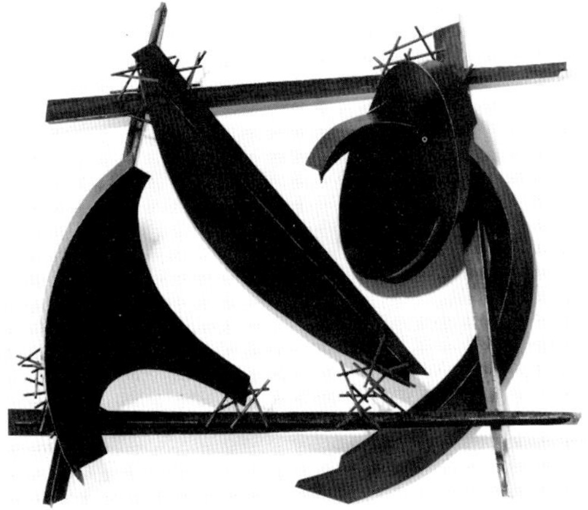

Fig. 70. *Wall Sculpture III*, 1979.

group that emphasized directness of expression as a primary virtue of painting.

We have seen how the development of the open space frame was based largely on the acknowledgment of the framing edges of painting. His involvement with the literal, flat frame of the 1956 wall relief *Sun, Moon, and Stars II* may have been the immediate stimulus for his first burst of large-scale painting since his early career. However, such is the intricate fusion of painting and sculpture in Ferber's work that we find the same all-over, broken tracery of *Sun, Moon, and Stars II* in the gem-like small painting on paper (fig. 71) executed in 1949. This kind of sequence, of working back and forth "as the sparrow goes," indicates that Ferber was not trying to translate sculptural problems into painting. "I was interested in two things," Ferber later recalled in speaking of the paintings of 1959-1963,

one, color, just color, and two, the elusiveness and challenge of capturing an image. In sculpture you don't capture an image — you work on it for months, making a few changes. In painting you can change the whole surface in half an hour and start over again. . . . In painting, you can actually see the image go. You may have something, barely a suggestion, and if you don't capture it, you've lost it. This never happens in sculpture.[79]

Ferber kept his color in the earliest of these paintings within a muted range of black, white, and dark greens and browns, but by the early sixties the hues had become brighter and the values higher-keyed to include reds and yellows, although the overall palette never was brilliant. The shapes — the image — relate to his sculptures of the time but establish a distinct iden-

tity. In the paintings of 1958-1959 (fig. 72), for example, the undulating forms call to mind the roof sculptures of 1957 while also looking ahead to the *Sculpture as Environment*, but they always are broader than the shapes in the sculptures. One of painting's advantages was the ability to introduce this degree of broadness without an equivalent gain in weight or mass. These curving, rolling forms touch and push against — and at times even seem suspended from — the edges of the canvas in ways that also recall the roofed sculptures as well as the cages. In others the forms are more discontinuous and move and break more quickly, reminding us of the *Calligraph* sculptures of the time. However, the edges are often more irregular in the paintings, and their figure-ground relationship gives far more of a floating quality than do the sculptures. In the early sixties, the development of the paintings parallels the course of his sculpture — the number of forms in a given painting is reduced, and they become still broader and simpler, with a greater degree of openness (fig. 73). We now find two wide calligraphs that have coalesced into half-circles and that elide into a disk which usually is placed in either of the upper corners. In this sense his paintings aligned with post-painterly developments at an earlier date than his sculpture. In fact, his experience with painting in all likelihood helped to prepare him to engage his sculpture with the new vocabulary.

The large-scale paintings that emerged in 1973 can be traced to 1970. At that time Ferber began to incorporate brilliant, intense colors that saturated the entire field of the drawings he did for freestanding sculptures (fig. 74). The reds, yellows, blues, and whites that enveloped these drawings had no precedent in his work. Their appearance signaled the emer-

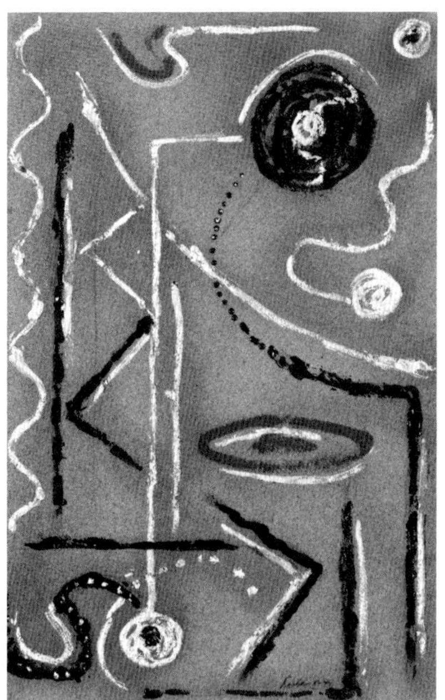

Fig. 71. Untitled, August 1949.

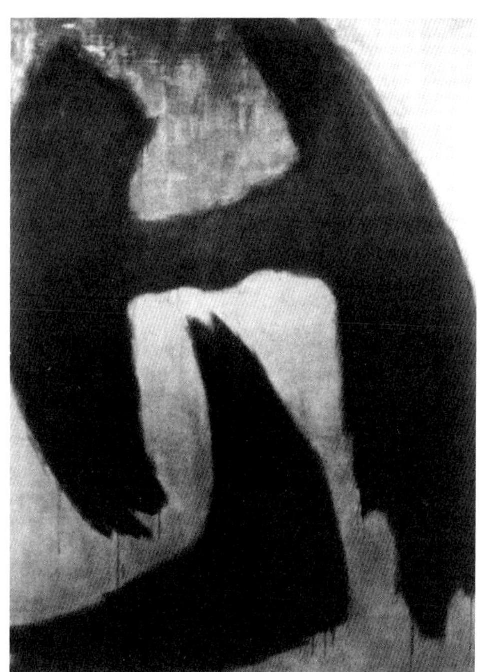

Fig. 72. *Rutgers #5*, 1959.

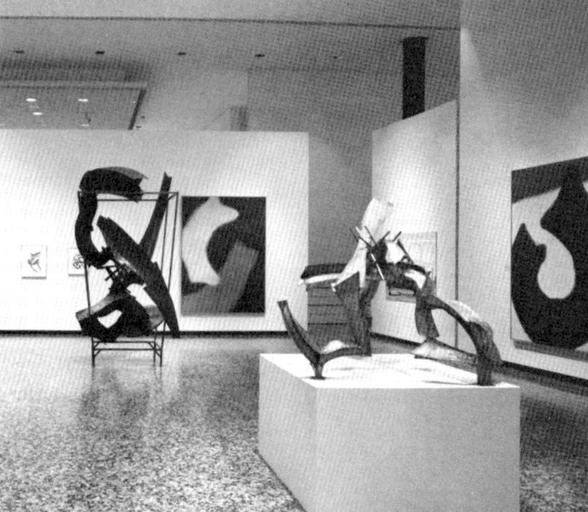

Fig. 73. Installation photograph. *Herbert Ferber: Sculpture, Painting, Drawing 1945-1980.* The Museum of Fine Arts, Houston.

gence of the primary characteristic of the post-1973 paintings, for it is color that Ferber now sees as his greatest challenge in painting. Shapes became geometric and were far less important to the carrying of the painting. At first, they were based on a zigzag pattern, but since then Ferber has reversed his normal course and has made the shapes more complex, although they still serve primarily as a means to carry color on surfaces. Geometric shapes first appeared in small paintings on paper (fig. 75) of 1971 and 1972. These were divided into irregular quadrants which call to mind the way in which Noland's off-centered chevrons of 1964 cut into the field. In two cases a quadrant contained horizontal bands, and in another work he used a saw-toothed pattern that had been suggested to him by a North American Indian rug that he owned. It was this pattern, made far simpler and extended from one or both of the painting's edges, that Ferber settled on as the motif for the large-scale paintings. How these paintings are read depends to great extent on just how Ferber places and adjusts the pattern in the field. Considerable differences in the format also are attained by modifying the size, scale, and angle of the saw teeth or by introducing a small triangle that juts into the field from the bottom edge. (color plate V).

But color carries these paintings, and in their sheer intensity Ferber seems to have made up for long years of working only with the primarily neutral colors of the sculptor's materials. His hues run the spectrum from high-pitched reds and oranges to deep blacks, from purple to green to grays and browns. They sometimes are closely gradated in hue and value, but in others they are contrasted starkly and separated widely in the spectrum. Colors almost always bleed into one another,

but at points the patterns stand apart sharply, at others they seem almost to fuse in a heavy veiled atmosphere. Increasingly, other and often contrasting colors are brushed and run into the broad primary areas, creating a highly painterly, scumbled, and brushed effect. At this time Ferber had eliminated all vestiges of painterly surfaces in his sculpture. However, his deeply ingrained Expressionist side apparently missed them, thus perhaps accounting for their reappearance in the paintings.

In 1977 Ferber began to cut out and lift a triangle from the surface and reattach it with the point of the triangle folded under to reveal the other side of its surface. Ferber's intent was to give himself more surfaces to work with and to employ several juxtaposed colors on contrasting surfaces. When one triangle is raised, he has four different surfaces, and when he began to cut out two triangles in 1979, even more surface effects were made possible. This process also established a far more complex and ambitious spatial interplay; our eye constantly shifts back and forth between real and illusionary space. Thin, poured lines, usually of a contrasting color, that move across two or even three different areas of color and space were introduced in 1979. These lines give an even greater spatial ambiguity while also helping to tie the various fields together in a coherent whole.

Ferber readily acknowledges that this format is not new, and he points to the raised paintings of Max Ernst and to Lucio Fontana's cut paintings as rough parallels to his work. However, he distinguishes his paintings from Fontana's, for example, in that unlike Fontana he uses the cut only as a point of departure. Ferber does not feel the raised surfaces are a sculptural phenomenon, but one cannot avoid comparing them to

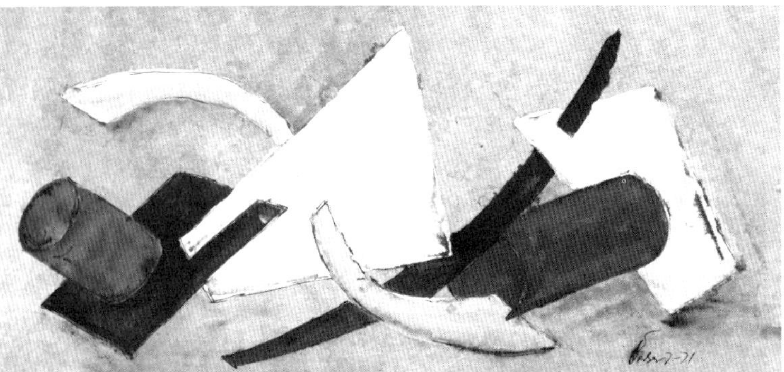

Fig. 74. Untitled, July 1971.

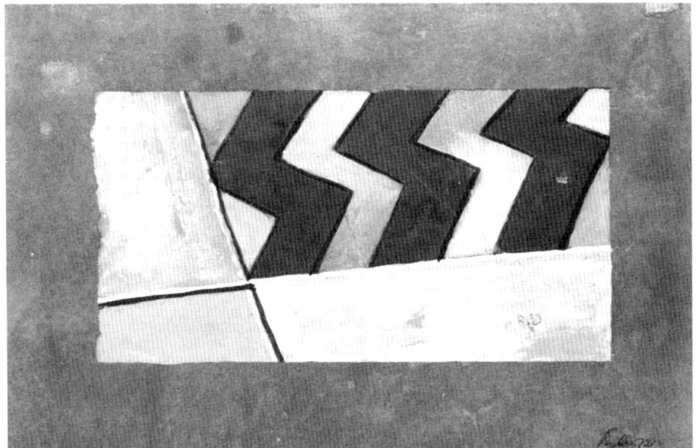

Fig. 75. Untitled, 1972.

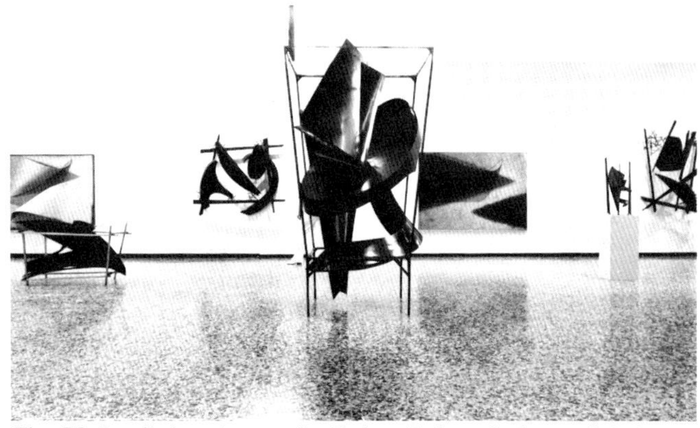

Fig. 76. Installation photograph. *Herbert Ferber: Sculpture, Painting, Drawing 1945-1980.* The Museum of Fine Arts, Houston.

the open, conical sections that Ferber also had introduced in his sculpture in 1977 in works such as *Canaan II* and that became a standard element in his work. The raised triangles in the paintings give a shape and substance that is, finally, sculptural in character and that was not found in the paintings of 1973 to 1977 (figs. 76-79 and color plate VIII). Cut and raised elements appear in sculptures such as *Orcivale,* 1978, and a roughly triangular shape, not unlike that in the paintings, is found in *Wall Sculpture I* of 1979. The wall sculptures may have been inspired to some extent by the paintings, much as the wall sculptures of 1956 anticipated the painting campaign launched in 1958. Such relationships reveal once again the close dialogue between painting and sculpture in Ferber's art. It also is worth noting the relationship between the raised surfaces of Ferber's paintings and recent wall reliefs with similar elements in the relief sculptures of the Russian Constructivists such as Ivan Puni and Uril Annenkov, as well as Archipenko, Tatlin, and Gabo. *The Planar Dimension,* organized at The Solomon R. Guggenheim Museum, impressed Ferber and was the largest of several shows in the 1970s that revived interest and established knowledge of these artists.[80] It is likely, however, that these artists confirmed and encouraged Ferber in a formal usage that he had established independently.

In the fall of 1981, Ferber introduced a vertical format for the raised paintings. He did this first simply by turning a horizontal painting on its side, then conceiving and executing them as distinctly vertical. The clearly vertical format was established by introducing a black diagonal band to create two separate and contrasting fields, one a warm color, the other a cool, which can be connected by the flap curving over from one field to the next. He now is consciously using richer, more deeply resonant colors as a result of looking at Old Master paintings, especially Memling and Van Eyck, on a trip to Holland and Belgium in the late fall of 1981. More recently, a brilliant clarity of color suggests the paintings of Piero della Francesca which Ferber saw on a trip to Florence in the fall of 1982.

Yet at the same time, Ferber could look back, as he has in his sculpture, to his earlier work, to re-explore older ideas and practices that could add fresh dimensions to his art. In 1982, for example, shapes in his paintings have come to recall those found in the calligraphic paintings of 1959-1962, an effect achieved by the removal of the point from the cut-out element, turning it into a convex shape of the older vocabulary. He again has taken to the American Surrealist practice of using lines from Shakespeare for the titles of some of his paintings, just as he sometimes did (along with Joyce's *Ulysses*) with his sculptures of the late forties.[81] He now is concentrating almost totally on painting, but his wealth of ideas for sculpture shows no sign of abating, as is made clear by the superb wash drawings of the last few years (figs. 80 and 91). Here, the sculptures stand in vast, unlimited, and imaginary fields of space that evoke the drawings of the mid and late 1940s. Although the sculptures in these drawings are rendered in his new planar idiom, they seem almost to function with an inner life in ways that distantly, yet insistently, recalls the large hybrid creatures in his Surrealist drawings. Has he, in some way, come full circle? We cannot yet know; but we do know that this exhilarating fusion of the old and new will continue to lead us to authentic, convincing art.

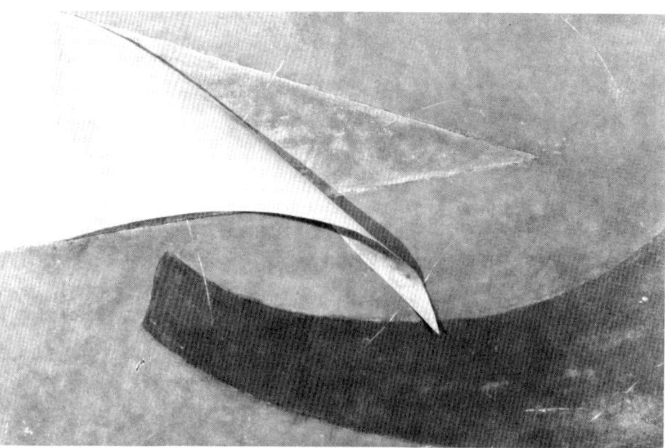
Fig. 78. *Jug End*, 1981.

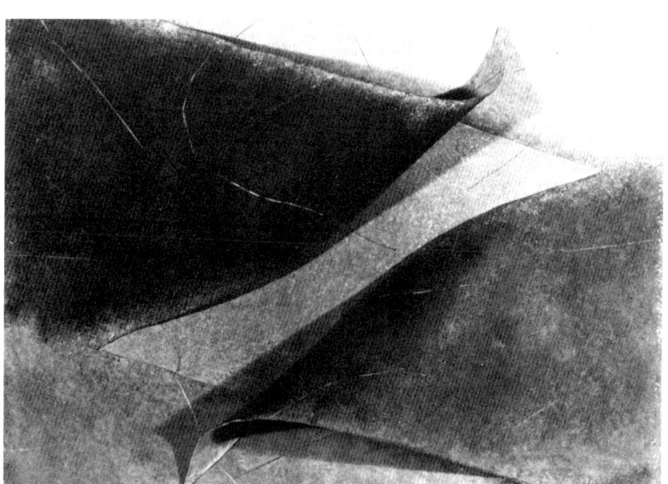
Fig. 77. *Troilus*, 1980.

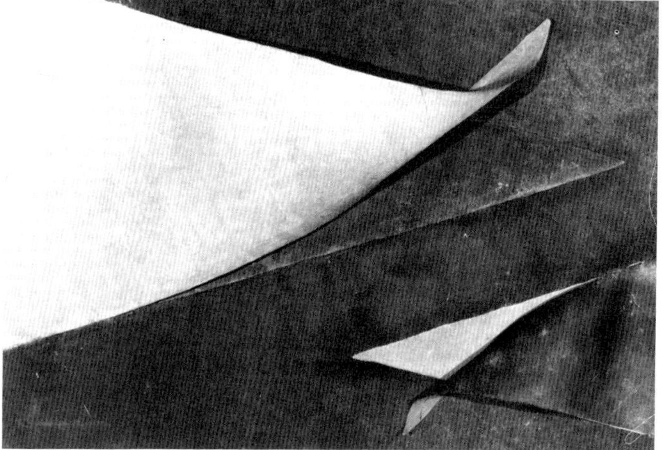
Fig. 79. *When Yellow Leaves*, 1981.

Abbreviations of Source Material

Andersen, 1961
Andersen, Wayne. Transcript of unpublished interview with Herbert Ferber. Archives of American Art, New York and Washington, D.C., September 1961.

Andersen, 1962
Andersen, Wayne. Exhibition catalogue *The Sculpture of Herbert Ferber* (Minneapolis: Walker Art Center, 1962).

Andersen, Environmental Sculpture
Andersen, Wayne. "Herbert Ferber: Environmental Sculpture." *Art International*, vol. 6 (September 1962), p. 24ff.

Andersen, American Sculpture
Andersen, Wayne. *American Sculpture in Process: 1930/1970* (Boston: New York Graphic Society, 1975).

Goossen, 1959
Goossen, Eugene C. "Herbert Ferber," in *Three American Sculptors: Ferber, Hare, Lassow,* with R. Goldwater and I. Sandler (New York: Grove Press, Inc., 1959).

Goossen, 1981
Goossen, Eugene C. *Herbert Ferber.* Chronology and bibliography by Phyllis Tuchman (New York: Abbeville Press, 1981).

Rubin
Rubin, William S. "Herbert Ferber's Sculpture in the Seventies," *Art International,* vol. 20 (February-March 1976), pp. 28-33.

Sandler
Sandler, Irving. Transcript of unpublished interviews with Herbert Ferber. Archives of American Art, New York and Washington, D.C., April 22, 1968; December 31, 1968; and January 9, 1969.

Footnotes

[1] In 1949, Clement Greenberg, in "The New Sculpture," *Partisan Review,* vol. 16 (June 1949), pp. 637-642 (reprinted in *Art and Culture* [Boston: Beacon Press, 1961], pp. 139-145), saw sculpture as having more potential than painting. By 1956, however, in his article, "David Smith," *Art in America,* vol. 44 (Winter 1956-1957), p. 306 (reprinted in *Art and Culture,* pp. 203-207), he stated that sculpture, with the exception of David Smith's, was a "general disappointment."

[2] I am grateful to Robert Miller, New York, for suggesting the parallel with Hofmann.

[3] Barbara Rose, *American Painting: The Eighties; A Critical Interpretation* (New York: Grey Art Gallery, 1979), p. 9.

[4] *Rubin*, p. 28.

[5] *Ibid.,* pp. 28-29.

[6] Darby Bannard, *Hans Hofmann: A Retrospective Exhibition* (Houston: The Museum of Fine Arts, Houston, and Washington, D.C.: The Hirshhorn Museum and Sculpture Garden, 1976), p. 11.

[7] Among other sculptors who studied there were Ibram Lassaw, 1930-1931; Phillip Pavia, 1930-1933; and Gabe Kohn, 1930-1934.

[8] Most of the facts of his life and career have been reported by Ferber to Phyllis Tuchman and are included in the chronology reprinted in this catalogue. They also were recorded extensively in *Sandler.* See also the chronology by Lucy Lippard in *Andersen, 1962,* pp. 53-54. Other aspects have been discussed with the author over the past five years.

[9] In a talk entitled "Twenty-Five Years of Sculpture," Bennington College, October 15, 1955; transcript in the Archives of American Art.

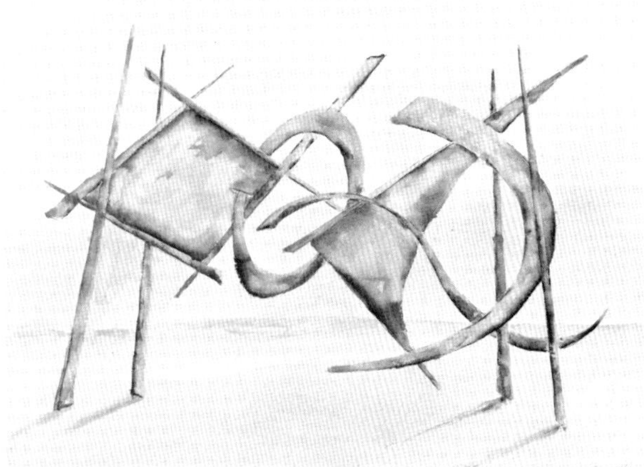

Fig. 80. Untitled, November 1979.

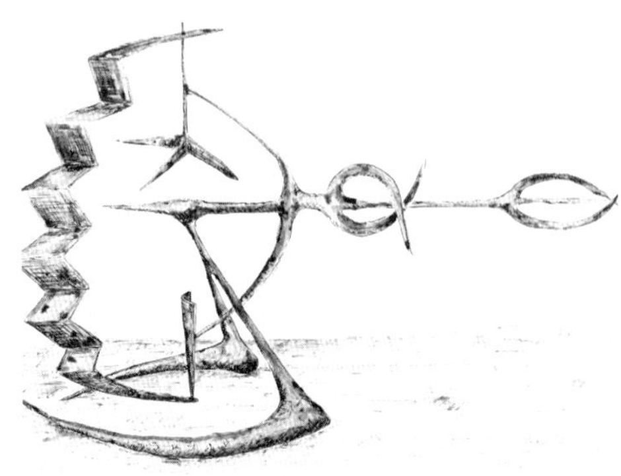

Fig. 82. Untitled, 6/50.

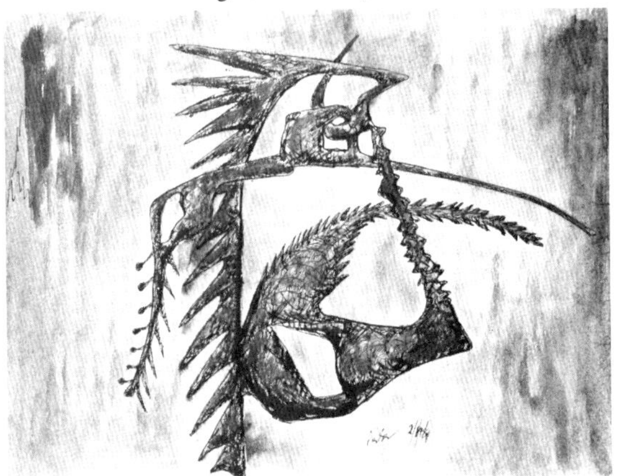

Fig. 81. Untitled, 2/1/48.

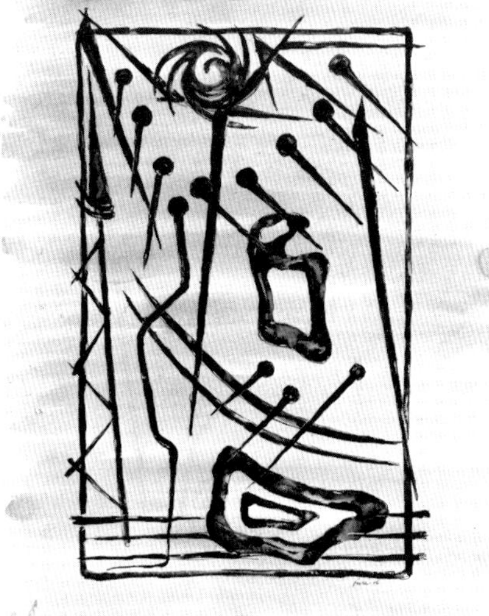

Fig. 83. Untitled, 1956.

---

[10]George Grey Barnard (1863-1938) was a sculptor, art collector, and dealer whose large and powerful neo-classic marble sculpture, *The Struggle of the Two Natures of Man* of 1894, is in the collection of The Metropolitan Museum of Art. Curiously, its theme suggests that found in Ferber's work at the time. He collected medieval sculpture extensively and put his collection on public display. It eventually was purchased for the Cloisters and the Philadelphia Museum of Art by John D. Rockefeller.

[11]*Sandler*, p. 6.

[12]*Ibid.*, p. 8.

[13]*Ibid.*, p. 7.

[14]In a video interview taped by the Albright-Knox Art Gallery, 1978, month and day unknown.

[15]*Henry Moore: Sculpture and Drawings*, introduction by Herbert Read (New York: Curt Valentin, 1944).

[16]*Sandler*, pp. 9-10.

[17]The Moore book contained drawings for completely open work, entitled *Imaginary Sculptures*, but Ferber does not remember seeing them.

[18]These goals often have been repeated by Ferber in talks and written statements. They were described first in *Andersen, 1962*, pp. 15-16.

[19]Julio Gonzalez, "Picasso Sculpteur," *Cahiers d'Art*, vol. 11, nos. 6-7 (1936), pp. 189-191.

[20]*Andersen, American Sculpture* gives an excellent chronicle of the sequence and technical development of this history for all the sculptors of Ferber's generation.

[21]See especially Ferber's statement in "The Ides of Art: Sculptors Write," *Tiger's Eye*, no. 4 (June 1948), p. 75.

[22]Interview with the author, April 28, 1969.

[23]*Sandler*, p. 37.

[24]See James Johnson Sweeney, *Alexander Calder* (New York: The Museum of Modern Art, 1951), and Bernice Rose, *Alexander Calder in the Collection of The Museum of Modern Art* (New York: The Museum of Modern Art, 1969).

[25]See Barbara Rose, Judith McCandless, and Duncan McMillan, *Miró in America* (Houston: The Museum of Fine Arts, Houston, 1982).

[26]Interview with the author, February 23, 1982.

[27]David Smith, "Abstract Art," *The New York Artist*, vol. I, no. II (April 1940), p. 15.

[28]For Smith's development and an excellent discussion of his move to fuse painting and sculpture, see Edward F. Fry, *David Smith* (New York: The Solomon R. Guggenheim Museum, 1969).

[29]*Andersen, 1962*, p. 15.

[30]*Ibid.*, p. 16.

[31]*Andersen, 1961*, p. 7.

[32]*Sandler*, p. 16.

[33]Ferber talk, "The Artist's Point of View," given at the Federation of Modern Painters and Sculptors Second Annual Forum, New York, April 23, 1947. Transcript in Ferber papers, Archives of American Art.

[34]*Andersen, American Sculpture*, p. 70.

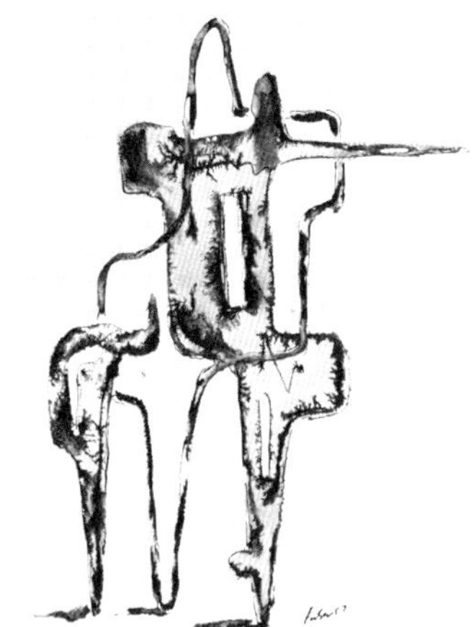

Fig. 84. *Study for Three*, 1957.

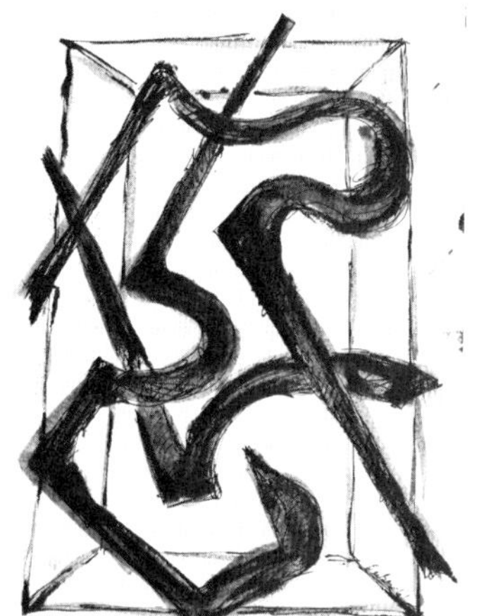

Fig. 86. Untitled, 1961.

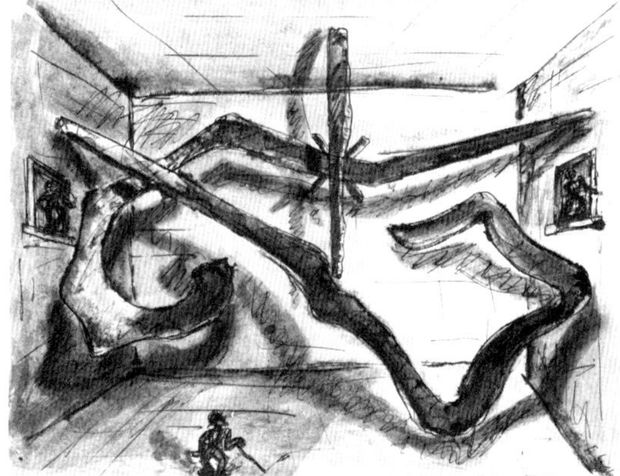

Fig. 85. Untitled, 1960.

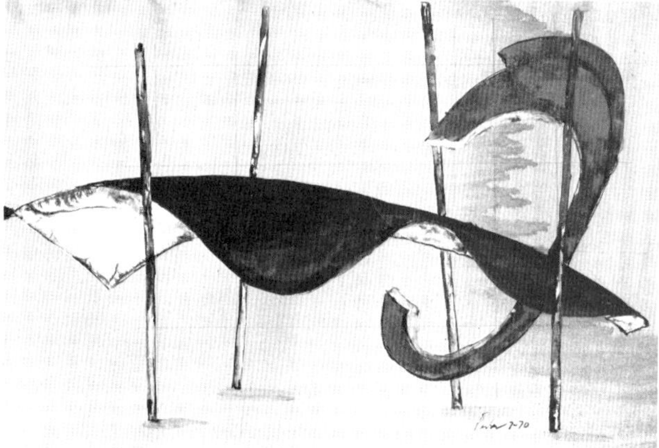

Fig. 87. Untitled, 7/70.

---

[35] Ferber statement in "The Ides of Art: The Attitudes of 10 Artists on Their Art and Contemporaneousness," *Tiger's Eye*, no. 2 (December 1947), p. 44. Ferber's reference to the artist working in an "arena" predates Harold Rosenberg's use of the term by five years in his famous article, "The American Action Painters," *Art News*, vol. 51 (December 1952), pp. 22-23.

[36] *Goossen, 1959*, p. 8.

[37] Ferber refers to these in *Andersen, 1961*, p. 35, by saying he was "perhaps unconsciously or intuitively representing bones, teeth, breasts, etc. I don't doubt I was trying to abstract these ideas and bring them into a sculptured form."

[38] *Goossen, 1959*, p. 11, describes it as a "skeletal condor," and *Goossen, 1981*, p. 65, as a "birdlike force."

[39] See Fry, *David Smith, op. cit.*, p. 53.

[40] Interview with the author, February 23, 1982.

[41] *Goossen, 1959*, p. 11, first made this point.

[42] See *Andersen, American Sculpture*, esp. pp. 6-87.

[43] Ferber talk, "Twenty-Five Years of Sculpture," *op. cit.*

[44] *Andersen, 1961*, pp. 15-16.

[45] This first was suggested in *Andersen, Environmental Sculpture*, p. 24.

[46] Ferber statement in Dorothy Miller, ed., *15 Americans* (New York: The Museum of Modern Art, 1952), p. 10.

[47] See Donald Judd, *Complete Writings, 1959-1975* (Halifax: The Press of the Nova Scotia College of Art and Design, and New York: New York University Press, 1975). See also William C. Agee, "Donald Judd: Unit, Series, Site," *Art in America*, vol. 63 (May-June 1975), pp. 40-49.

[48] John McCoubrey, *American Tradition in Painting* (New York: George Braziller, 1963).

[49] *Goossen, 1959*, pp. 13-14.

[50] Ferber referred to this in *Andersen, 1961*, pp. 24-25.

[51] Ferber statement, *15 Americans, op. cit.*

[52] For Ferber, the calligraph is not related to oriental art; as he views it, the calligraph represents the action of the eye, hand, and mind in following the form and indicates that the form has movement. See *Sandler*, p. 56.

[53] See *Andersen, American Sculpture*, pp. 6-87.

[54] See Fry, *David Smith, op. cit.*, p. 62.

[55] Robert Goldwater, *Herbert Ferber: First Retrospective Exhibition* (Bennington, Vermont: Bennington College, 1958), p. 2.

[56] *Goossen, 1981*, pp. 98-111.

[57] Ferber statement in *15 Americans, op. cit.*

[58] Ferber statement, *Tiger's Eye*, 1948, *op. cit.*

[59] E.C. Goossen, "The Big Canvas," *Art International*, vol. II (November 1958), pp. 45-47.

[60] *Goossen, 1981*, p. 102.

[61] Herbert Ferber, "Sculpture as Environment," *Art International*, vol. 4 (May 1, 1960), p. 71.

[62] In *Andersen, 1961*, p. 28, Ferber stated, "The four uprights of the cages define space as surely as a two-dimensional frame." This also was pointed out in *Rubin*, p. 33.

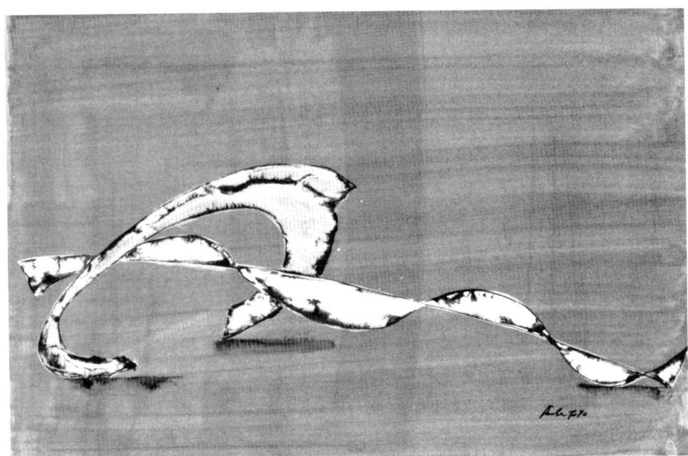

Fig. 88. Untitled, 1970.

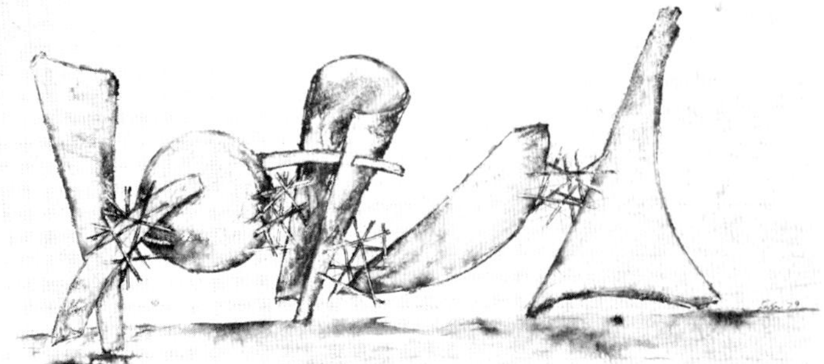

Fig. 90. Untitled, 1979.

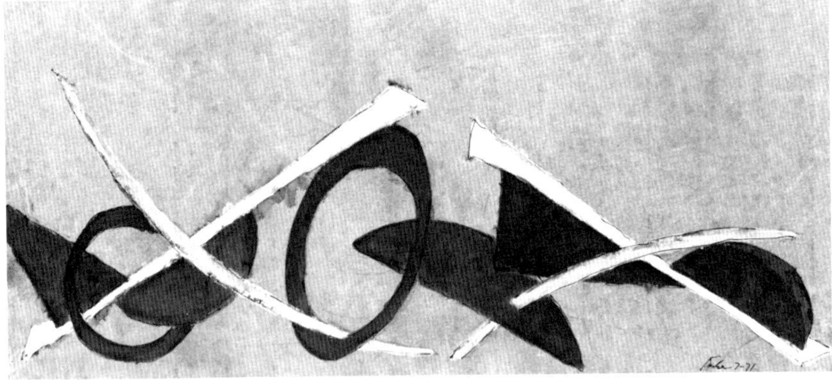

Fig. 89. Untitled, 1971.

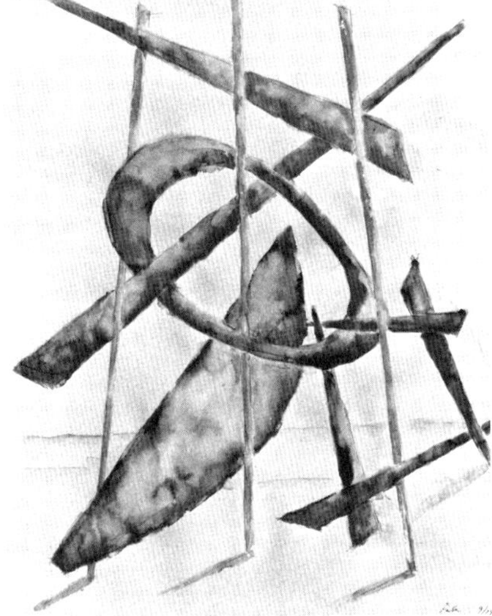

Fig. 91. Untitled, 9/79.

---

[63]*Rubin*, p. 29.

[64]*Ibid.*

[65]Transcript of untitled talk given at the Art Department, The University of Texas at Austin, December 10, 1979. Copies in possession of the artist and the author.

[66]See Fry, *David Smith, op. cit.*, p. 129.

[67]*Rubin*, p. 29.

[68]First pointed out in *Rubin*, pp. 29-30.

[69]Herbert Ferber, untitled statement in *Art Now: New York*, vol. 3 (March 1971), no pagination.

[70]Letter to the author, January 15, 1973.

[71]*Andersen, 1961*, p. 33.

[72]Interview with the author, April 28, 1981.

[73]Herbert Ferber, "The Schism Between the Artist and the Public," *The League Quarterly* (Summer 1949), pp. 18-20. Ferber dwelled on the question of the artist and society in his public lectures and seminars while he was visiting professor at Rice University in the fall of 1979.

[74]See, for example, the transcript of talk given by Ferber at the Architectural League in 1950, month and date unclear, for a forum organized by Philip Johnson and transcript of talk given at the symposium on "The New Sculpture," February 12, 1952, at The Museum of Modern Art, New York. Copies in the Archives of American Art.

[75]*Sandler*, p. 18.

[76]Phyllis Tuchman, "Interview with Herbert Ferber," *Artforum*, vol. 11 (March 1971), p. 57.

[77]Interview with the author, February 23, 1982. This and subsequent information on the paintings are drawn primarily from this and other discussions with the artist over the last two years.

[78]Ferber statement, *Tiger's Eye*, 1948, *op. cit.*

[79]Tuchman, *op. cit.*

[80]See, for example, the following exhibition catalogues:

Russian Art of the Revolution. Foreword by Thomas W. Leavitt, introduction by Sarah Bodine (Ithaca, New York: Andrew Dickson White Museum of Art, Cornell University, 1970).

Art in Revolution: Soviet Art and Design since 1917. Introduction by Camilla Gray-Prokofieva (London: Hayward Gallery, 1971).

Russian Avant-Garde: 1908-1922. Foreword by S. Frederick Starr, Essay by John E. Bowlt (New York: Leonard Hutton Galleries, 1971).

[81]A sculpture of 1949 was entitled *If I Touch Them They Bleed* (Collection Philip Johnson, New Canaan, Connecticut); a painting of 1981 is called *To the Noble Mind II* (Private collection, New York). See *Andersen, 1961*, p. 40.

Public Collections

Albright-Knox Art Gallery, Buffalo, New York

Bennington Museum, Bennington, Vermont

Centre Georges Pompidou, Paris

Cranbrook Academy of Art, Bloomfield Hills, Michigan

The Detroit Institute of Arts

Grand Rapids Art Museum, Michigan

The Metropolitan Museum of Art, New York

The Museum of Fine Arts, Houston

The Museum of Modern Art, New York

National Gallery of Art, Washington, D.C.

The Newark Museum, Newark, New Jersey

New York University, New York

Norton Simon Museum of Art at Pasadena, California

Rutgers University Art Gallery, New Brunswick, New Jersey

The Solomon R. Guggenheim Museum, New York

Storm King Art Center, Mountainville, New York

University of Indiana, Bloomington

University of Vermont, Burlington

Walker Art Center, Minneapolis

Whitney Museum of American Art, New York

Williams College Museum of Art, Williamstown, Massachusetts

Yale University Art Gallery, New Haven, Connecticut

One-Man Exhibitions

Midtown Galleries, New York, 1937, 1943

Betty Parsons Gallery, New York, 1947, 1950, 1953

Samuel Kootz Gallery, New York, 1955, 1957

Herbert Ferber: First Retrospective Exhibition, Bennington Museum, Vermont, 1958

Columbia University School of Architecture, 1960

André Emmerich Gallery, New York, 1960, 1963, 1965, 1967, 1969, 1970, 1972, 1974, 1975, 1976, 1977

Sculpture of Herbert Ferber, Walker Art Center, Minneapolis; Des Moines Art Center; San Francisco Museum of Modern Art; Dallas Museum for Contemporary Arts; The Santa Barbara Museum of Art, California; Whitney Museum of American Art, New York, 1962-1963

University of Vermont, Burlington, 1964

Dag Hammarskjöld Plaza Sculpture Garden, New York, 1972

Sculpture and Painting by Herbert Ferber, Roy Boyd Gallery, Chicago, 1978

M. Knoedler & Co., Inc., New York, 1978, 1979, 1980

Herbert Ferber: Sculpture, Painting, and Drawing 1945-1980, The Museum of Fine Arts, Houston and the Des Moines Art Center, 1981-1982.

Chronology

by Phyllis Tuchman

1906
Born Herbert Ferber Silvers on April 30 in New York City, only child of Hattie (née Lebowitz) and Louis Silvers, typesetter and trade school printing teacher.

1923
Graduates from Morris High School in the Bronx. Member of the soccer and rifle teams and school sports reporter for *New York Herald Tribune.* Close friend of William Phillips, later founder and co-editor of *Partisan Review;* through him later meets Clement Greenberg and Harold Rosenberg. Enters College of the City of New York.

1926
Majors in science and audits literature, philosophy, and art history courses. Member of swimming team. By special arrangement, leaves CCNY to enter Columbia University Dental School. Meets Barnett Newman; William Steig, later a *New Yorker* magazine cartoonist; and Jules Henry, anthropologist who later introduces him to Margaret Mead.

1927
Awarded B.S. by Columbia University while enrolled in the dental school. Enjoys anatomical drawing for dental classes and begins drawing from nature and from sculpture at The Metropolitan Museum of Art. During the next three years, studies sculpture at night at tuition-free, instructorless Beaux Arts Institute of Design, where Leo Lantelli and Edward McCarten occasionally critique students' figure studies.

1929
Awarded $25 fourth prize, Beaux Arts Competition, for a classical metope of Athena and Perseus with Medusa's head. Studies etching on his own.

1930
Awarded D.D.S. from College of Oral and Dental Surgery, Columbia University. Joins Columbia faculty as part-time instructor and establishes part-time dental practice. Studies for six months at National Academy of Design; expelled for doing nonacademic figurative sculpture, but then is reinstated. Exhibits landscape and figure etchings at National Arts Club. Also exhibits at National Academy of Design. Receives summer scholarship to work at Louis Comfort Tiffany Foundation, Oyster Bay, Long Island. While there, meets Ilya Bolotowsky and David McCosh, later head of University of Oregon art department. In autumn, shares studio with McCosh, who had been in Europe for a year, who painted in the manner of Cézanne, and who later introduces him to Theodore Roszak and other artists. Sees Guillaume Collection of African sculpture, a strong influence. Works on painting, etching, and sculpture, especially painting.

1931
Spends summer painting in Woodstock, New York, to which he returns several times. Buys his first African sculpture. Exhibits painting in group shows, Brooklyn Museum, Pennsylvania Academy of The Fine Arts (Philadelphia) *Annual Exhibition of Painting and Sculpture* (also 1942, 1943, 1945, 1946, 1954, 1958). Makes first wood carvings. Shows photographs of work to William Zorach and asks to study with him; Zorach advises him simply to purchase tools and materials and work on his own.

1932
Marries Dr. Sonia Stirt, psychoanalyst. Exhibits painting in group show, Corcoran Gallery of Art, Washington, D.C. By now is a serious sculptor, but continues his lifelong involvement with painting, watercolor, and colored drawing.

1933
Rents 61st Street studio in Lincoln Arcade and works there through 1943. Exhibits paintings in group shows at Philadelphia Art Alliance and Corcoran Gallery of Art, Washington, D. C.; and *Paintings, Sculpture, Drawings, Prints on the Theme Hunger-Fascism-War,* John Reed Club Gallery, New York. Works on wood and stone carvings. Begins to use Ferber, his middle name, as his artist's name.

1934
Coauthors scholarly paper for *Journal of Dental Research,* February. Meets Wassily Leontief, Nobel laureate in economics, through poet Estelle Leontief, a childhood friend. Also meets members of the Frankfurt School who had left Germany and had become associates at Columbia, including sociologists Leo Lowenthal and Herbert Marcuse and the philosopher Max Horkheimer, and attends their seminars.

1935
Leaves Kleeman and Hudson Galleries and joins Midtown Galleries. Exhibits sculpture in group show, Midtown Galleries. Drives to Mexico, first of several trips there. Buys pre-Columbian sculptures. Returns via Chicago and Stone City, Iowa, where he teaches stone carving at Grant Wood's school for two weeks.

1936
Exhibits sculpture in group show, Midtown Galleries. Participates in and exhibits at the First American Artists' Congress (also 1940). Joins the Artists' Union; attends talks by José Orozco and David Siqueiros there and at the John Reed Club.

1937
Has one-man show, Midtown Galleries, December 7-20. Featured in *Time* magazine article.

1938

Travels in Europe for two months during summer. Leaves Rome after short stay due to Fascist situation. In France, sketches Romanesque sculpture at Moissac, Carcassonne, and Souillac. Exhibits in group show at the Jeu de Paume, Paris, sponsored by and also later shown at The Museum of Modern Art, New York. Exhibits in group shows at The Baltimore Museum of Art; the Museum of Modern Art Gallery, Washington, D.C.; the Sculptors' Guild (also 1939-1942, 1948); and the Whitney Museum of American Art *Annual Exhibition of Contemporary American Painting and Sculpture* (also 1940, 1942, 1945, 1954, 1956-1960, 1964, 1966, 1968).

(Ferber showed sculpture in all exhibitions mentioned hereafter, except where noted.)

1939

Exhibits at the Golden Gate International Exposition, San Francisco.

1940

Exhibits at New York World's Fair. With Meyer Schapiro, Adolph Gottlieb, Mark Rothko, Ilya Bolotowsky, Bradley Walker Tomlin, David Smith, and others, founds Federation of Modern Painters and Sculptors as a splinter group from American Artists' Congress.

1941

Elected to executive board, Sculptors' Guild, along with Chaim Gross, Robert Laurent, and Hugo Robus. Shows at the *52nd Annual Exhibition of American Paintings and Sculpture*, The Art Institute of Chicago (also 1954).

1942

Awarded $1,000 Fifth Purchase Prize, The Metropolitan Museum of Art *Artists for Victory* exhibition.

1943

Has one-man show, Midtown Galleries, May 17-June 4. Divorces. Moves to penthouse studio-apartment on Riverside Drive.

1944

Marries Ilse Falk, historian of medieval art. Makes last wood sculptures.

1945

Draws abstract studies, but does no sculpture for almost a year, then begins again with semi-abstract work in various media. Rents house in Barton, Vermont; spends summers there until 1972.

1946

Joins Betty Parsons Gallery. Milieu includes members of adjacent Samuel Kootz Gallery. Becomes friendly with Jackson Pollock, Adolph Gottlieb, Robert Motherwell, Ad Reinhardt, William Baziotes, Bradley Walker Tomlin, Theodore Stamos, and particularly Mark Rothko. Participates in gathering of these artists along with Alfred Barr, Dorothy Miller, George Dennison, Meyer Schapiro, Robert Goldwater, Sam Hunter, E. C. Goossen, Herbert Marcuse, and Leo Lowenthal. Exhibits model of relief for exterior of Kleinhaus Music Hall, Buffalo, in *Architecture Needs Sculpture* at the Sculptors' Guild, his first work in architectural sculpture.

1947

Has one-man show, Betty Parsons Gallery, December 15, 1947 - January 3, 1948. Participates in the Art Students League Second Annual Forum. Exhibits in *Abstract and Non-Objective Sculpture*, Clay Club Sculpture Center.

1948

Elected full member, Kappa Chapter (Columbia University), Society of Sigma Psi. August-October, travels in England, where he visits Henry Moore and spends time with composer Richard Arnell; France (through Burgundian Romanesque region); and Italy, where he studies Donatello's Campanile *Prophets*. Participates in Studio 35 activities. Exhibits in *Sculpture at the Crossroads* (Henry Rox, organizer), Worcester (Massachusetts) Art Museum.

1949

Presents talk at Subjects of the Artist School and speaks on panel at the Art Students League Fourth Annual Forum.

1950

Has one-man show, Betty Parsons Gallery, March 6-25, installation designed by Tony Smith. Joins "The Irascibles" in a protest against a juried painting exhibition at The Metropolitan Museum of Art. Featured in *Life* magazine. Presents talk at the New York Architectural League. Charter member, The Club.

1951

The Museum of Modern Art purchases *Jackson Pollock*. Exhibits in *I. Sao Paolo Biennal*, Brazil; *Abstract Painting and Sculpture in America* (Andrew Carnduff Ritchie, curator), The Museum of Modern Art; and *9th Street Show* (Leo Castelli, organizer). Commissioned together with Gottlieb and Motherwell for art for B'nai Israel Synagogue in Millburn, New Jersey.

1952

Robert Goodnough publishes "Ferber Makes a Sculpture" in

Art News, November. Exhibits in *15 Americans* (Dorothy Miller, curator), The Museum of Modern Art (others include Baziotes, Richard Lippold, Pollock, Rothko, Clyfford Still, and Tomlin). Participates in The Museum of Modern Art's "Symposium on the New Sculpture" with David Smith, Lippold, and Roszak. *". . . And the bush was not consumed,"* begun March 1951, installed at B'nai Israel Synagogue (Percival Goodman, architect); assisted by Tony Louvis, assembles work in Day Schnabel's studio.

1953
Has one-man show, Betty Parsons Gallery, April 20 - May 9. Award winner, Unknown Political Prisoner Monument Competition (Andrew Ritchie, Perry Rathbone, Seymour Swarzenski, jurors); subsequent showings at The Museum of Modern Art and the Tate Gallery, London.

1954
Designs light and candelabrum for Berlin Chapel, Brandeis University (Max Abramowitz, architect). Participates in panel, College Art Association Annual Meeting, Philadelphia. Makes first roofed sculptures which led to sculpture as environment, 1959-1961.

1955
Has one-man show, Samuel Kootz Gallery, January 25 - February 12. Participates in "Symposium on Art and Music," Bennington College (Vermont). Exhibits in *The New Decade: 35 American Painters and Sculptors* (John I.H. Baur, curator), Whitney Museum of American Art; exhibition travels to San Francisco, Los Angeles, St. Louis, and Denver. Devotes considerable amount of time to painting for the next three years.

1956
Robert Goldwater writes on Ferber for *Cimaise* magazine, Paris/New York. Meets William S. Rubin, then professor of art history, Sarah Lawrence College.

1957
Has one-man show, Samuel Kootz Gallery, December 3 - 21. Two interior wall sculptures installed, Temple Anshe Chesed, Cleveland (Percival Goodman, architect). Exhibits in *Irons in the Fire*, Contemporary Arts Museum, Houston (Sam Hunter, curator).

1958
Retrospective exhibition, Bennington College (E. C. Goossen, director; Robert Goldwater, catalogue introduction). Exhibits at Brussels World's Fair, U.S. Pavillion, in *Carnegie International*, Pittsburgh, and *Nature in Abstraction* (John I. H. Baur, curator), Whitney Museum of American Art. In summer, concentrates on painting large canvases.

1959
Three American Sculptors, with text on Ferber by E. C. Goossen, published. Exhibits in *Documenta II*, Kassel, West Germany. Begins to make maquettes of *Sculpture as Environment*. Also concentrates on large paintings.

1960
Has one-man painting show, André Emmerich Gallery, January 5 - 23. Has one-man show, Avery Hall, School of Architecture, Columbia University. Lectures on "Sculpture as Environment," Princeton University and Columbia School of Architecture. Exhibits in *Aspects de la sculpture américaine*, Galerie Claude Bernard, Paris.

1961
Exhibits *Sculpture as Environment*, commissioned by Whitney Museum of American Art. Participates in symposium at the New School for Social Research.

1962
Retrospective exhibition organized by Wayne V. Andersen for the Walker Art Center, Minneapolis; exhibition travels to Des Moines, San Francisco, Dallas, Santa Barbara, and the Whitney Museum of American Art, New York. Visiting professor of art, University of Pennsylvania. Exhibits in *Sculptures in the City*, Festival of Two Worlds, Spoleto; *American Art Since 1950* (Sam Hunter, curator), Seattle World's Fair; *A Survey of American Sculpture: Late 18th Century to 1962* (William Gerdts, curator), The Newark Museum; and "Art in Embassies" program, Warsaw.

1963
Has one-man show, André Emmerich Gallery, April 2 - 20. Commissioned by Harlow Carpenter to design full-scale outdoor sculpture and architecture as an environment, Waitsfield, Vermont (project is unrealized). Juror, *54th Annual Exhibition*, Museum of Art, Carnegie Institute, Pittsburgh. Exhibits in *Sculpture in the Open Air*, Battersea Park, London.

1964
Has one-man show, Robert Hull Fleming Museum, University of Vermont, Burlington. Juror, sculpture exhibition, National Gallery of Canada, Ottawa. Exhibits at the New York World's Fair and in *Between the Fairs: 25 Years of American Art* (John I. H. Baur, curator), Whitney Museum of American Art.

1965
Has one-man show, André Emmerich Gallery, January 5-23. Moves Studio to 825 Broadway. Visiting professor of sculpture, Rutgers University, through 1967. Rutgers University commissions 18-foot sculpture for Commons Building. Participates in the White House Festival of the Arts. Exhibits in

Etats-Unis, sculptures du XXe siècle, Musée Rodin, Paris, sponsored by the International Council of The Museum of Modern Art; exhibit travels to Berlin and Baden-Baden.

1966

Sculpture as Environment installed in Ferber Lounge, Rutgers University. Juror, *Sculpture '66,* University of Illinois, Chicago. Participates in sculpture symposium at The University of Texas, Austin, with Louis Kahn, James Rosati, and George McNeil. Exhibits in *Art of the United States: 1670-1966,* Whitney Museum of American Art, celebrating opening of new building, and *7 Decades: 1895-1965* (Peter Selz, organizer), Public Education Association, New York.

1967

Has one-man show, André Emmerich Gallery, February 11 - March 2. Associate fellow, Morse College, Yale University. Divorces. Marries Edith Popiel.

1968

Installs *Full Circle,* John F. Kennedy Federal Building, Government Center, Boston. Tapes interview for Archives of American Art with Irving Sandler. Temporary installation of *Three Arches* at Fifth Avenue and 59th Street. Exhibits in *Dada, Surrealism, and Their Heritage* (William S. Rubin, curator), The Museum of Modern Art, and at HemisFair '68, San Antonio.

1969

Awarded a Guggenheim Fellowship. Exhibits in *The New American Painting and Sculpture: The First Generation* (William S. Rubin and William C. Agee, curators) and *Nelson Aldrich Rockefeller Collection of 20th-Century Art,* both at The Museum of Modern Art.

1970

Has one-man show, André Emmerich Gallery, November 14 - December 2. Moves household and studio to MacDougal Street. Delivers eulogy at his friend Mark Rothko's funeral. Appointed guardian for daughter Kate Rothko and executor of estate of Mrs. Mark Rothko.

1972

Has one-man show, André Emmerich Gallery, November 11 - 29. Has one-man show, Hammarskjöld Plaza, New York, May - July. Purchases house and studio in Berkshires, North Egremont, Massachusetts, for summers and holidays. Initiates Rothko lawsuit on behalf of Kate Rothko.

1973

Installs 22-foot-high sculpture, American Dental Association headquarters building, Chicago. Exhibits in *American-Type Sculpture* (Phyllis Tuchman, curator), School of Visual Arts Gallery, New York, and in *Sculpture of the '50s,* Santa Barbara Museum of Art.

1974

Publishes Gottlieb obituary, *New York Times.* Exhibits in *Monumenta* (Sam Hunter, curator), Newport, Rhode Island.

1975

Has one-man show, André Emmerich Gallery, January 11-29. Has one-man painting show, André Emmerich Gallery, September 17 - October 8. Participates in panel discussion, School of Visual Arts, with Ibram Lassaw, Joel Perlman, Peter Reginato, and Tuchman. Visits Egypt.

1976

Exhibits in *200 Years of American Sculpture* (in section organized by Rosalind E. Krauss), Whitney Museum of American Art.

1977

Has one-man painting show, André Emmerich Gallery, February 26 - March 16. Gives up part-time dental practice; continues to teach part-time at Columbia University Dental School. Tours Greece with Leontiefs.

1978

Has one-man shows, M. Knoedler and Co., Inc., April 1-20, and Roy Boyd Gallery, Chicago, November 3 - December 6. Installs 18-foot sculpture commissioned in 1977 by city of Ottumwa, Iowa. Included in *Masters of Modern Sculpture, Part Three,* a Michael Blackwood film. Exhibits in *Painting and Sculpture Today,* Indianapolis Museum of Art, June 12 - July 30, and in *Art for Collectors,* The Toledo Museum of Art, November 12 - December 17.

1979

Has one-man show, M. Knoedler and Co., Inc. March 10-29. Awarded R. S. Reynolds Memorial Award for aluminum sculpture for 1979. Exhibits in *Vanguard American Sculpture: 1913-1939* at Rutgers University. Occupies Mellon Chair in the Humanities at Rice University, Houston, in fall.

1980

Has one-man show, M. Knoedler and Co., Inc., April 19 - May 10.

1981

Retrospective exhibition at The Museum of Fine Arts, Houston, May 1 - June 28, and Des Moines Art Center, November 23, 1981 - January 3, 1982.

Checklist

Sculpture

1 *Three-Legged Woman II.* 1945
Bronze cast made from lead original in 1981.
24 x 18 x 18 in. (61 x 45.7 x 45.7 cm.)
Lent by Herbert Ferber,
Courtesy of M. Knoedler & Co., Inc.,
New York

*2 *Metamorphosis I.* 1946
Bronze. 6 x 12 x 6 in.
(15.3 x 30.5 x 15.3 cm.)
Lent by Edith Ferber, New York

3 *Hazardous Encounter.* 1947
Bronze. 22 x 36 x 15 in.
(55.9 x 91.5 x 38.1 cm.)
Lent by Herbert Ferber,
Courtesy of M. Knoedler & Co., Inc.,
New York

4 *Labors of Hercules.* 1948
Bronze. 35 x 24 x 12 in.
(88.9 x 61 x 30.5 cm.)
Lent by Edith Ferber, New York

5 *Jackson Pollock.* 1949
Lead. $17\frac{5}{8}$ x 30 x 10 in.
(44.8 x 76.2 x 25.4 cm.)
Lent by The Museum of Modern Art,
New York,
Purchase, 1949

6 *Horned Sculpture.* 1949 and 1957
Bronze cast made from lead original in 1969.
74 x 15 x 12 in. (188 x 38.1 x 30.5 cm.)
Lent by The Museum of Fine Arts, Houston,
Museum purchase with funds provided by the
National Endowment for the Arts, Mr. and
Mrs. George R. Brown, and Mr. George
S. Heyer, Jr. 79.1

7 *He Is Not a Man.* 1950
Bronze with welded metal rods (unique cast
made from lead original in 1969). $67\frac{1}{4}$ x
$19\frac{1}{2}$ x $13\frac{3}{8}$ in. (170.9 x 49.4 x 33.9 cm.)
Lent by The Museum of Modern Art,
New York,
Gift of William Rubin, 1971.

8 *Calligraph II.* 1950 and 1953
Lead and copper. 78 x 24 x 18 in.
(198.5 x 61 x 46 cm.)
Lent by Herbert Ferber,
Courtesy of M. Knoedler & Co., Inc.,
New York

9 *The Bow.* 1950
Bronze cast made from lead, brass, and
copper original in 1969. 47 x $30\frac{1}{8}$ x $24\frac{1}{8}$
in. (119.3 x 76.5 x 61 cm.)
(Includes bronze base, 1 x $11\frac{3}{8}$ x $13\frac{7}{8}$ in.
[2.5 x 38.9 x 35.2 cm.])
Lent by The Museum of Modern Art,
New York,
Given anonymously, 1969

10 *Spheroid II.* 1952
Copper, brass, and lead. 42 x 33 x 47 in.
(106.7 x 83.8 x 119.4 cm.)
Lent by Richard L. Rubin, Bedford,
New York

*11 *Green Sculpture II.* 1954
Copper. $40\frac{1}{2}$ x 42 x 24 in.
(102.8 x 106.7 x 61 cm.)
Lent by Albright-Knox Art Gallery, Buffalo,
Gift of Seymour H. Knox, 1957

12 *Roofed Sculpture with S Curve II.* 1954
Bronze. 50 x 60 x 22 in.
(127 x 152.4 x 55.9 cm.)
Lent by Herbert Ferber,
Courtesy of M. Knoedler & Co., Inc.,
New York

13 Model for *Sculpture as Environment* based on
Roofed Sculpture with S Curve II. 1954 and
1958 Bronze. $13\frac{5}{8}$ x $16\frac{3}{4}$ x $8\frac{1}{2}$ in.
(34.6 x 42.5 x 21.6 cm.)
Lent by Herbert Ferber,
Courtesy of M. Knoedler & Co., Inc.,
New York

14 *Sun, Moon, and Stars II.* 1956
Brass. 71 x 46 x $10\frac{1}{4}$ in.
(180.3 x 116.8 x 26 cm.)
Lent by the Whitney Museum of American
Art, New York,
Gift of The Howard and Jean Lipman Founda-
tion, Inc., 1965. 65.64

15 *Sun Wheel.* 1956
Brass, copper, and stainless steel. $56\frac{1}{4}$ x 29 x
19 in. (142.9 x 73.7 x 48.3 cm.)
Lent by the Whitney Museum of American
Art, New York. 56.18

16 *Calligraph with Sloping Roof, Two Walls II.*
1957 and 1963
Copper. 45 x 52 x 22 in.
(114.4 x 132.1 x 55.9 cm.)
Lent by Edith Ferber, New York

17 *Flags II.* 1957
Brass and copper. $54\frac{3}{4}$ x 26 x 15 in.
(139.8 x 66.1 x 38.1 cm.)
Lent by The Prudential Insurance Company
of America, Newark, New Jersey

18 *Calligraph LC.* 1959
Brass. $58\frac{1}{4}$ x $28\frac{1}{2}$ x $8\frac{1}{2}$ in.
(147.9 x 72.4 x 21.6 cm.)
Lent by Herbert Ferber,
Courtesy of M. Knoedler & Co., Inc.,
New York

*19 Model for *Rutgers Environment. (Sculpture as
Environment.)* 1960
Mesh wire coated with plaster and painted,
wire cage, painted wood base. $18\frac{7}{8}$ x 23 x
$32\frac{3}{4}$ in. (47.9 x 58.4 x 83.2 cm.)
Lent by Rutgers University Art Gallery,
New Brunswick, New Jersey
Gift of the artist

*20 *Homage to Piranesi IIa.* 1962-1963
Copper. 90 x $46\frac{1}{2}$ x $46\frac{1}{2}$ in.
(228.6 x 118.1 x 118.1 cm.)
Lent by The Metropolitan Museum of Art,
New York,
Gift of William Rubin, 1965

21 *Homage to Piranesi IIIc.* 1963
Copper and brass. 104 x 65 x 65 in.
(264.1 x 165.1 x 165.1 cm.)
Lent by Rutgers University Art Gallery, New
Brunswick, New Jersey,
Gift of the artist

22 *Three Arches II.* 1964
Copper. 48 x 63 x 57 in.
(121.9 x 160 x 144.8 cm.)
Lent by Herbert Ferber,
Courtesy of M. Knoedler & Co., Inc.,
New York

*23 *Homage to Piranesi IVc.* 1964
Copper. 110 x 58 x 87 in.
(279.4 x 142.3 x 221 cm.)
Lent by Edith Ferber, New York

24 *Calligraph Double One on C Ia.* 1964
Copper. $28\frac{1}{4}$ x $7\frac{1}{2}$ x 7 in.
(71.7 x 19.1 x 17.8 cm.)
Private collection, Houston

25 *Homage to Piranesi Ve.* 1965 and 1966
Copper and brass. $96\frac{1}{2}$ x $57\frac{3}{8}$ x $67\frac{1}{8}$ in.
(245.2 x 145.7 x 170.5 cm.)
Lent by the National Gallery of Art,
Washington, D.C.,
Gift of William S. Rubin, 1977

26 *Calligraph Sept. 10, '66 III.* 1966
Copper. 73 x 62 x $19\frac{1}{2}$ in.
(185.5 x 157.5 x 49.5 cm.)
Private collection, Houston

*27 *Calligraph Nov. '66 III*. 1966-1968
  Copper. 76 x 56 x 36 in.
  (193.1 x 142.3 x 91.4 cm.)
  Lent by Mr. and Mrs. Robert Postal,
  Great Neck, New York

*28 *Two Squares II*. 1968
  Copper. 131 x 79 x 66 in.
  (332.7 x 200.6 x 167.6 cm.)
  Lent by the Whitney Museum of American
  Art, New York,
  Gift of Mr. and Mrs. Monroe Geller,
  1974. 74.33

 29 *Bill's Discovery*. 1969
  Cor-Ten steel. 27 x 63 x 21 in.
  (68.6 x 160 x 53.3 cm.)
  Lent by Herbert Ferber,
  Courtesy of M. Knoedler & Co., Inc.,
  New York

 30 *Newport III*. 1969
  Cor-Ten steel and brass. 91 x 67 x 75 in.
  (231.2 x 170.2 x 190.5 cm.)
  Lent by Abrams Family Collection, New York

*31 *Two Squares with Disk II*. 1970
  Cor-Ten steel and brass. 138 x 72 x 72 in.
  (350.5 x 182.9 x 182.9 cm.)
  Lent by Herbert Ferber,
  Courtesy of M. Knoedler & Co., Inc.,
  New York

*32 *Mt. Holly II*. 1970
  Cor-Ten steel. 40 x 78 x 60 in.
  (101.6 x 198.5 x 152.4 cm.)
  Lent by Herbert Ferber,
  Courtesy of M. Knoedler & Co., Inc.,
  New York

*33 *Homage to Piranesi VII 1 (Oval and Triangle
  in Cage)*. 1970-1971
  Cor-Ten steel and brass. 50 x 30 x 30 in.
  (127 x 76.2 x 76.2 cm.)
  Lent by Edith Ferber, New York

*34 *Pico II*. 1971
  Cor-Ten steel. 49 x 78 x 78 in.
  (124.5 x 198.5 x 198.5 cm.)
  Lent by Herbert Ferber,
  Courtesy of M. Knoedler & Co., Inc.,
  New York

*35 *Three Poles I*. 1971
  Copper. 20 x 14 x 16 in.
  (50.8 x 35.5 x 40.6 cm.)
  Lent by Herbert Ferber,
  Courtesy of M. Knoedler & Co., Inc.,
  New York

*36 *Cone II*. 1971-1972
  Cor-Ten steel. 56 x 120 x 48 in.
  (142.3 x 304.8 x 121.9 cm.)
  Lent by Herbert Ferber,
  Courtesy of M. Knoedler & Co., Inc.,
  New York

 37 *Konkapot II*. 1971-1972
  Cor-Ten steel. 69 x 48 x 118 in.
  (175.4 x 121.9 x 299.7 cm.)
  Lent by Storm King Art Center, Mountain-
  ville, New York,
  Purchased with aid of funds from the
  National Endowment for the Arts

 38 Model for *Egremont II*. 1971-1972
  Copper. 12 x 26 x 9 in.
  (30.5 x 66 x 22.9 cm.)
  Private collection, Norwood, New Jersey

*39 *MacDougal III*. 1972-1974
  Cor-Ten steel. 48 x 120 x 48 in.
  (121.9 x 304.8 x 121.9 cm.)
  Lent by Herbert Ferber,
  Courtesy of M. Knoedler & Co., Inc.,
  New York

*40 *Peru I*. 1973
  Cor-Ten steel. 44 x 78 x 71 in.
  (111.8 x 198.5 x 180.4 cm.)
  Lent by Herbert Ferber,
  Courtesy of M. Knoedler & Co., Inc.,
  New York

*41 *Richmond II*. 1974
  Cor-Ten steel. 60 x 120 x 48 in.
  (152.4 x 304.8 x 121.9 cm.)
  Lent by Herbert Ferber,
  Courtesy of M. Knoedler & Co., Inc.,
  New York

 42 *Furnace II*. 1974 and 1976
  Cor-Ten steel. 48 x 120 x 60 in.
  (121.9 x 304.8 x 152.4 cm.)
  Lent by Georges Pompidou Art & Culture
  Foundation, New York

 43 *Lenox II*. 1975
  Brass. 72 x 120 x 72 in.
  (182.9 x 304.8 x 182.9 cm.)
  Lent by Murray Financial Corporation, Dallas

*44 *Pisgah II*. 1976
  Brass. 52 x 72 x 48 in.
  (132.1 x 182.4 x 121.9 cm.)
  Lent by Sharon and Neil Norry,
  Rochester, New York

*45 *Williams IIIa*. 1976
  Steel. 76 x 112 x 70 in.
  (193.1 x 284.5 x 177.8 cm.)
  Lent by Herbert Ferber,
  Courtesy of M. Knoedler & Co., Inc.,
  New York

*46 *Cleft II*. 1977-1978
  Steel and brass. 36 x 54 x 36 in.
  (91.4 x 137.2 x 91.4 cm.)
  Lent by Congregation Beth Israel, Houston

*47 *Canaan II*. 1977-1978
  Steel. 59 x 110 x 52 in.
  (149.9 x 279 x 132.2 cm.)
  Lent by Herbert Ferber,
  Courtesy of M. Knoedler & Co., Inc.
  New York

*48 *Homage to Piranesi IXa*. 1977-1978
  Brass. 139 x 68 x 61 in.
  (353.1 x 172.7 x 154.9 cm.)
  Lent by Herbert Ferber,
  Courtesy of M. Knoedler & Co., Inc.,
  New York

 49 *Notch View*. 1978
  Steel. 76 x 144 x 76 in.
  (193.1 x 365.8 x 193.1 cm.)
  Lent by Diane and Steve Jacobson,
  East Hampton, New York

 50 *Orcivale*. 1978
  Brass. 40½ x 36 x 36 in.
  (102.9 x 91.4 x 91.4 cm.)
  Lent by Mr. and Mrs. Fulton Murray, Dallas

*51 *Velay*. 1978
  Brass. 35 x 19 x 16 in.
  (88.9 x 48.2 x 40.6 cm.)
  Lent by Mr. and Mrs. Robert Pergament,
  Kings Point, New York

 52 *Homage to Piranesi X. (Sens)* 1978
  Steel. 40 x 24½ x 21½ in.
  (101.6 x 62.2 x 54.6 cm.)
  Lent by Herbert Ferber,
  Courtesy of M. Knoedler & Co., Inc.,
  New York

*53 *Baldwin Hill*. 1979
  Steel. 87 x 38 x 45 in.
  (221 x 96.5 x 114.3 cm.)
  Lent by Herbert Ferber,
  Courtesy of M. Knoedler & Co., Inc.,
  New York

 54 *Chesterwood*. 1979
  Steel. 78 x 132 x 48 in.
  (198.5 x 335.5 x 121.9 cm.)
  Lent by Herbert Ferber,
  Courtesy of M. Knoedler & Co., Inc.,
  New York

55 *Four Poles.* 1979
Steel. 61 x 54 x 38 in.
(154.9 x 137.2 x 96.5 cm.)
Lent by Herbert Ferber,
Courtesy of M. Knoedler & Co., Inc.,
New York

*56 *Wall Sculpture I.* 1979
Steel. 63¼ x 72 x 40 in.
(160.7 x 182.9 x 101.6 cm.)
Lent by Herbert Ferber,
Courtesy of M. Knoedler & Co., Inc.,
New York

*57 *Wall Sculpture III.* 1979
Steel. 63 x 48 x 38½ in.
(160 x 121.9 x 97.8 cm.)
Private collection, Houston

58 *Wall Sculpture 2.* 1980
Steel. 75 x 48 x 28 in.
(190.5 x 121.9 x 71.1 cm.)
Lent by Herbert Ferber,
Courtesy of M. Knoedler & Co., Inc.,
New York

Works on Paper

(All works on paper, except where noted, are lent
by Herbert Ferber, courtesy of M. Knoedler &
Co., Inc., New York.)

1 Untitled. 1946
Pen and ink and wash on paper. 10⁵⁄₁₆ x 8 in.
(26.2 x 20 cm.)
Lent by The Museum of Fine Arts, Houston,
Gift of Mr. and Mrs. Harvey Bott in memory
of Gene Von Stoffler. 78.244

2 Study for *Metamorphosis.* May 1947
Gouache and pen and ink on tracing paper.
9 x 11⅝ in. (22.7 x 29.4 cm.)
Lent by The Museum of Modern Art,
New York,
Gift of the artist

3 Untitled. February 1, 1948
Gouache, pen and ink, and wash on paper.
9½ x 12⅜ in. (24.1 x 31.4 cm.)

4 Untitled. August 1949
Gouache on paper. 20¼ x 13⅛ in.
(51.4 x 33.3 cm.)

5 Study for *Jackson Pollock.* January 1949
Gouache, brush, and pen and ink on buff
paper. 8½ x 13¾ in. (21.3 x 34.6 cm.)
Lent by The Museum of Modern Art,
New York,
Gift of the artist

6 Study for *Calligraph II* and related to *He Is
Not a Man* and *Flame.* August 1949
Wash, pencil, and pen and ink on paper.
18½ x 8¾ in. (47 x 22.3 cm.)
Lent by The Museum of Modern Art,
New York,
Gift of the artist

7 Untitled. June 1950
Pen and ink and wash on paper.
18⅝ x 24½ in. (47.3 x 62.2 cm.)

8 Untitled. July 2, 1950
Pen and ink and wash on paper.
18¹¹⁄₁₆ x 24½ in. (48.1 x 62.2 cm.)

9 Study for *The Bow.* July 1950
Wash and pen and ink on paper.
18¾ x 12½ in. (47.4 x 31.5 cm.)
Lent by The Museum of Modern Art,
New York,
Gift of the artist

10 Untitled. 1956
Pen and ink and wash on paper. 24 x 19 in.
(61 x 48.3 cm.)

11 Study for *Three.* 1957
Pen and ink and wash on paper.
15½ x 11¼ in. (39.3 x 28.6 cm.)

12 Untitled. 1958
Ink on paper. 15¼ x 11⅛ in.
(38.7 x 28.2 cm.)

*13 Untitled. 1958
Oil on paper. 13¾ x 8⅞ in. (34.9 x 22.5 cm.)

14 *Calligraph.* 1959
Brush and ink on gray paper. 20⅛ x 12⅞ in.
(51.4 x 32.6 cm.)
Lent by The Museum of Modern Art,
New York,
Gift of the artist

15 *Calligraph.* 1959
Wash, brush, and ink on gray paper.
20⅛ x 12⅞ in. (51.1 x 32.5 cm.)
Lent by The Museum of Modern Art,
New York,
Gift of the artist

16 *Calligraph with Two Walls.* 1961
Wash, brush, pen and red ink, and charcoal.
20¼ x 13¾ in. (51.1 x 34.6 cm.)
Lent by The Museum of Modern Art,
New York,
Gift of the artist

17 Study for *Sculpture as Environment,*
developed from *Roof Sculpture with S Curve
II.* 1960
Wash and pen and ink on gray paper.
20 x 25⅝ in. (50.7 x 64.9 cm.)
Lent by The Museum of Modern Art,
New York,
Gift of the artist

18 Study for *Sculpture as Environment.* 1960
Wash and pen and ink on paper.
30¼ x 22¼ in. (76.8 x 56.2 cm.)
Lent by The Museum of Modern Art,
New York,
Gift of the artist

*19 Untitled. 1960
Ink wash on paper. 27 x 40½ in.
(68.6 x 102.9 cm.)

20 Untitled. 1961.
Pen and ink and ink wash on paper.
13⅝ x 10⅛ in. (34.6 x 25.7 cm.)

21 Untitled. 1961
Pen and ink and wash on paper.
18⅞ x 13½ in. (47.9 x 34.3 cm.)

22 Study after *Calligraph in Cage with Cluster*
and *Homage to Piranesi.* 1961.
Wash, pen and ink, and charcoal on paper.
20¼ x 13⅝ in. (51.2 x 34.6 cm.)
Lent by The Museum of Modern Art,
New York,
Gift of the artist

23 *Sculpture to Make an Environment.*
July 18, 1962
Pen and ink and wash on paper. 19 x 25 in.
(48.3 x 63.5 cm.)

*24 Untitled. August 13, 1962
Pen and ink and wash on paper.
15½ x 23¹⁄₁₆ in. (39.4 x 58.6 cm.)

*25 Untitled. May 23, 1962
Ink wash on paper. 7⅜ x 5⅞ in.
(18.7 x 14.9 cm.)

26 Study for *Cage* series. May 23, 1962
Charcoal and brush and ink on paper.
22⅜ x 14¼ in. (56.8 x 36.2 cm.)
Lent by The Museum of Modern Art,
New York,
Gift of the artist

*27 Untitled. May 28, 1962
Ink wash on paper. 7⅜ x 5⅞ in.
(18.7 x 14.9 cm.)

*28 Untitled. May 28, 1962
Ink wash on paper. 7⅜ x 5⅞ in.
(18.7 x 14.9 cm.)

*29 Untitled. May 28, 1962
Ink wash on paper. 7⅜ x 5⅞ in.
(18.7 x 14.9 cm.)

30 Untitled. 1964
Ink wash on paper. 24⅝ x 18⅝ in.
(62.5 x 47.3 cm.)
Private collection, Houston

31 Untitled. 1966
Wash, pen and ink, and charcoal on paper.
34⅝ x 18¾ in. (62.5 x 50.2 cm.)
Lent by The Museum of Modern Art,
New York,
Gift of the artist

32 Untitled. July 1970
Gouache, pen and ink, and wash on paper.
10 x 12¾ in. (25.4 x 32.4 cm.)

33 Untitled. July 1970
Gouache and pen and ink on paper.
10 x 11½ in. (25.4 x 29.2 cm.)

34 Untitled. July 1970
Gouache and ink on paper. 12⅞ x 19 in.
(32.7 x 48.3 cm.)

35 Untitled. 1970
Ink and gouache on paper. 12¾ x 20 in.
(32.4 x 50.8 cm.)

*36 Untitled. July 1971
Gouache, and pen and ink wash on paper.
9 x 19¼ in. (22.9 x 48.9 cm.)

*37 Untitled. July 1971
Pen and ink, gouache, and wash on paper.
9 x 19½ in. (22.9 x 49.5 cm.)

*38 Untitled. 1971
Gouache and ink wash on paper.
10⅝ x 16 in. (27 x 40.6 cm.)

*39 Untitled. 1972
Gouache on paper. 9¹³⁄₁₆ x 15⅛ in.
(24.9 x 38.4 cm.)

*40 Untitled. 1972
Gouache on paper. 11 x 24 in. (27.9 x 61 cm.)

*41 Untitled. 1974
Ink wash and watercolor on paper.
19⅝ x 24½ in. (49.8 x 62.2 cm.)

42 Untitled. August 1974
Ink, wash, and gouache on paper.
24½ x 39¼ in. (62.2 x 99.7 cm.)

*43 Untitled. 1979
Ink wash and crayon on paper.
10½ x 22½ in. (26.7 x 57.2 cm.)

*44 Untitled. April 1979
Ink, wash, pencil, and crayon on paper.
11³⁄₁₆ x 15 in. (28.4 x 38.1 cm.)

*45 Untitled. July 1979
Pen and ink, wash, and crayon on paper.
13³⁄₁₆ x 13 in. (33.5 x 33 cm.)

*46 Untitled. September 1979
Pen and ink, wash, and gouache on paper.
25⁵⁄₁₆ x 19½ in. (64.3 x 49.5 cm.)

*47 Untitled. November 1979
Watercolor, ink wash, and crayon on paper.
22¼ x 30 in. (56.5 x 76.2 cm.)

Paintings

(All paintings, except where noted, are lent by
Herbert Ferber, courtesy of M. Knoedler & Co.,
Inc., New York.)

Section I. 1959-1963

*1 *Rutgers No. 5.* 1959
Oil and magna on canvas. 90½ x 78½ in.
(229.9 x 171.4 cm.)

2 *Rutgers No. 6.* 1959
Oil and magna on canvas. 80 x 60 in.
(203.2 x 152.4 cm.)

*3 *Rutgers No. 16.* 1962-1963
Oil and magna on canvas. 68 x 90 in.
(172.7 x 228.6 cm.)

*4 *Black Gee.* 1963
Oil and magna on canvas. 90 x 73⅝ in.
(228.6 x 187.1 cm.)

Section II. 1974-1980

1 *Sausage and Peppers.* 1974
Synthetic polymer paint on canvas.
54 x 89 in. (137.1 x 226.1 cm.)

2 *Presidio.* 1974
Synthetic polymer paint on canvas.
55½ x 80 in. (141 x 203.2 cm.)

*3 *Purple Passage.* 1974
Synthetic polymer paint on canvas.
63 x 112 in. (160 x 284.4 cm.)

4 *Blue Lightning.* 1974
Synthetic polymer paint on canvas.
65 x 114 in. (165.1 x 289.5 cm.)

*5 *Deep Blue.* 1974
Synthetic polymer paint on canvas.
67 x 90 in. (170.2 x 228.6 cm.)

6 *Event Horizon.* 1975
Synthetic polymer paint on canvas.
84 x 129 in. (213.4 x 327.7 cm.)

*7 *Reflection IV.* 1976
Synthetic polymer paint on canvas.
60 x 110 in. (152.4 x 279.4 cm.)

*8 *Julien.* 1976
Synthetic polymer paint on canvas.
60 x 88¾ in. (152.4 x 225.4 cm.)

9 *Taconic.* 1979
Synthetic polymer paint and wire mesh
on canvas. 55 x 82 x 14 in.
(139.7 x 210.8 x 35.6 cm.)
Private collection, New York

*10 *Becket.* 1979
Synthetic polymer paint on canvas.
54¾ x 83 x 15 in. (139 x 208.3 x 38.1 cm.)
Lent by Henry V. Heuser, Jr.,
Louisville, Kentucky

*11 *Pink.* 1979
Synthetic polymer paint on canvas.
60¼ x 90 x 13 in. (153 x 228.6 x 33 cm.)
Lent by The Museum of Modern Art,
New York,
Fractional gift of Mr. and Mrs. Herbert
Freedman, 1980

*12 *By Sea, By Land.* 1980
Synthetic polymer paint and wire mesh on
canvas. 62 x 90 x 15½ in.
(157.5 x 228.6 x 39.4 cm.)
Lent by Stephen B. Chase,
Rancho Mirage, California

13 *Unbolt the Gate.* 1980
Synthetic polymer paint and wire mesh on
canvas. 62 x 90 x 15 in.
(157.5 x 228.6 x 38.1 cm.)
Lent by Stephen B. Chase,
Rancho Mirage, California

Illustrations

1. *Torso*, 1932. Mahogany. 9½ x 4 x 3 in. (24.1 x 10.2 x 7.6 cm.) Edith Ferber.
2. *Wrestlers*, 1934. Butternutwood. 36 in. (91.4 cm.) Rutgers University Art Gallery. New Brunswick.
3. *Wrestlers*, 1936. 12 x 15 x 3 in. (30.5 x 38.1 x 7.6 cm.) Jack Daly, New York.
4. *To Fight Again*, 1937. Granite. 24 x 36 x 9 in. (60.9 x 91.4 x 58 cm.) Metropolitan Museum of Art, New York.
5. *Shadow of a Hero*, 1943. Bronze, 6 x 9½ x 7 in. (38.7 x 24.1 x 17.8 cm.) Edith Ferber.
6. *Reclining Woman I*, 1944. Bronze. 10 x 6 x 4 in. (25.4 x 15.2 x 10.2 cm.)
7. *Reclining Woman II*, 1945. Bronze 16 x 36 x 12 in. (40.6 x 91.4 x 30.5 cm.) Rutgers University Art Gallery.
8. Untitled, 1946. Pen and ink and wash. 10⁵⁄₁₆ x 8 in. (26.2 x 20.3 cm.) The Museum of Fine Arts, Houston. Gift of Mr. and Mrs. Harvey Bott in memory of Gene Von Stoffler.
9. *Three Legged Woman II*, 1945. Bronze cast from lead original in 1981. 24 x 18 x 18 in. (61 x 45.7 x 45.7 cm.)
10. *Seated Figure*, 1945. Lead. 13 in. (33.02 cm.)
11. *Mermaid*, 1946. Lead. 12 in. (30.48 cm.)
12. *Metamorphosis I*, 1946. Bronze. 6 x 12 x 6 in. (15.3 x 30.5 x 15.3 cm.) Edith Ferber.
13. *Act of Aggression II*, 1946. Lead. 15 in. (38.1 cm.)
14. *Hazardous Encounter*, 1947. Bronze. 22 x 36 x 15 in. (55.9 x 91.5 x 38.1 cm.)
15. *Surrational Zeus II*, 1947. Lead. 48 x 30 in. (121.92 x 76.2 cm.) Edith Ferber.
16. *Labors of Hercules*, 1948. Bronze. 35 x 24 x 12 in. (88.9 x 61 x 30.5 cm.) Edith Ferber.
17. *Jackson Pollock*, 1949. Lead. 17⅝ x 30 x 10 in. (44.8 x 76.2 x 25.4 cm.) The Museum of Modern Art, New York. Purchase, 1949.
18. *Manifestation II*, 1949. Lead. 26 x 36 in. (66 x 91.4 cm.) Grand Rapids Art Gallery, Grand Rapids, Michigan.
19. *The Action is the Pattern*, 1949. Lead and brass rods. 18 x 18 in. (45.7 x 45.7 cm.) Estate of Mary Alice Rothko.
20. *Flame*, 1949. Lead and brass rods. 60 in. (152.4 cm.) Whitney Museum of American Art, New York.
21. *Horned Sculpture*, 1949 and 1957. Bronze cast made from lead original in 1969. 74 x 15 x 12 in. (188 x 38.1 x 30.5 cm.) The Museum of Fine Arts, Houston. Museum purchase with funds provided by the National Endowment for the Arts, Mr. and Mrs. George R. Brown, and Mr. George S. Heyer, Jr. 79.1.

22. *He is Not a Man*, 1950. Bronze with welded metal rods. 67¼ in. (170.8 cm.) The Museum of Modern Art, New York. Gift of William Rubin.
23. *The Bow*, 1950. Bronze cast made from lead, brass, and copper original in 1969. 47 x 30⅛ x 24⅛ in. (119.3 x 76.5 x 61 cm.) The Museum of Modern Art, New York. Anonymous gift.
24. "*. . . and the bush was not consumed*," 1951. Soldered copper, brass, lead, and tin. 15 x 96 x 36 in. (386 x 243.8 x 91.4 cm.) Facade: B'nai Israel Synagogue, Millburn, New Jersey.
25. *Spheroid II*, 1952. Soldered lead, brass, and copper. 42 x 33 x 47 in. (106.7 x 83.8 x 119.4 cm.) Richard L. Rubin.
26. *Green Sculpture II*, 1954. Copper. 40½ x 42 x 24 in. (102.8 x 106.7 x 61 cm.) Albright-Knox Art Gallery, Buffalo. Gift of Seymour H. Knox, 1957.
27. *Roofed Sculpture with S Curve II*, 1954. Bronze. 50 x 60 x 22 in. (127 x 152.4 x 55.9 cm.)
28. *Sun, Moon, and Stars II*, 1956. Brass. 71 x 46 x 10¼ in. (180.3 x 116.8 x 26 cm.) The Whitney Museum of American Art, New York. Gift of The Howard & Jean Lipman Foundation, Inc., 1965.
29. *Sun Wheel*, 1956. Brass, copper, and stainless steel. 56¼ x 29 in. (142.9 x 73.7 cm.) Whitney Museum of American Art, New York.
30. *Flags II*, 1957. Brass and copper. 54¾ x 26 x 15 in. (139.8 x 66 x 38.1 cm.) The Prudential Insurance Company of America, Newark.
31. *Calligraph with Sloping Roof, Two Walls II*, 1957-1963. Brazed brass. 45 x 52 x 22 in. (114.3 x 132 x 55.9 cm.) Edith Ferber.
32. *Sculpture as Environment*, 1960-1961. Scale model II. 18⅞ x 23 x 32¾ in. (47.9 x 58.4 x 83.2 cm.) Rutgers University Art Gallery, New Brunswick.
33. *Sculpture as Environment*, 1968, as installed at Rutgers University, New Brunswick.
34. *Homage to Piranesi IIIc*, 1963. Copper and brass. 104 x 65 x 65 in. (264.1 x 165.1 x 165.1 cm.) Rutgers University Art Gallery, New Brunswick, Gift of the artist.
35. *Homage to Piranesi Ve*, 1965 and 1966. Copper and brass. 96½ x 57⅜ x 67⅛ in. (245.2 x 145.7 x 170.5 cm.) National Gallery of Art, Washington, D.C.
36. *Calligraph LC*, 1959. Brass 58¼ x 28½ x 8½ in. (147.9 x 72.4 x 21.6 cm.)
37. *Homage to Piranesi IVc*, 1964. Copper. 110 x 58 x 87 in. (279.4 x 142.3 x 221 cm.) Edith Ferber.
38. *Two Squares with Disk II*, 1970. Cor-Ten steel and brass. 138 x 72 x 72 in. (350.5 x 182.9 x 182.9 cm.)

39. *Calligraph Sept. 10, '66 III*, 1966. Copper. 73 x 62 x 19½ in. (185.5 x 157.5 x 49.5 cm.) Private Collection, Houston.
40. *Calligraph Nov. '66 III*, 1966-1968. Copper. 76 x 56 x 36 in. (193.1 x 142.3 x 91.4 cm.) Mr. and Mrs. Robert Postal, Great Neck, New York.
41. *Full Circle*, 1966. Copper. 12 x 18 x 10 in. (30.5 x 45.7 x 25.4 cm.) John F. Kennedy Office Bldg., Boston, Mass.
42. *Ray II*, 1969. Copper. 42 x 48 in. (106.7 x 121.9 cm.)
43. *Newport III*, 1969. Cor-Ten steel. 91 x 67 x 75 in. (231.2 x 170.2 x 190.5 cm.) Abrams Family Collection, New York.
44. *Burke II*, 1970. Cor-Ten steel. 102 x 76 in. (259 x 193.04 cm.) Bruce Gritlin, Brookville, Long Island.
45. *Mt. Holly II*, 1970. 40 x 78 x 60 in. 101.6 x 198.5 x 152.4 cm.)
46. *St. Johns II*, 1970. Cor-Ten steel. 36 x 92 in. (91.4 x 233.7 cm.)
47. *Two Rings II*, 1971. Cor-Ten steel. 58 x 72 x 42 in. (147.3 x 182.8 x 106.7 cm.)
48. *Cone II*, 1971-1972. Cor-Ten steel. 56 x 120 x 48 in. (142.3 x 304.8 x 121.9 cm.)
49. *Konkapot II*, 1971-1972. Cor-Ten steel. 69 x 48 x 18 in. (175.4 x 121.9 x 299.7 cm.) Storm King Art Center, Mountainville, New York, Purchased with aid of funds from the National Endowment of the Arts.
50. *Homage to Piranesi VII 1 (Oval and Triangle in Cage)*, 1970-1971. Cor-Ten steel and brass. 50 x 30 x 30 in. (127 x 76.2 x 76.2 cm.) Edith Ferber.
51. *Three Poles III*, 1971 and 1975. Cor-Ten steel. 185 x 144 in. (469.9 x 365.7 cm.) Mr. and Mrs. Milton Gilbert, Alpine, New Jersey.
52. *Pisgah II*, 1976. Brass. 52 x 72 x 48 in. (132.1 x 182.4 x 121.9 cm.) Sharon and Neil Norry, Rochester, New York.
53. *Cleft II*, 1977-1978. Steel and brass. 36 x 54 x 36 in. (91.4 x 137.2 x 91.4 cm.) Congregation Beth Israel, Houston.
54. *Egremont II*, 1971-1972. Cor-Ten steel. 105 x 252 in. (266.7 x 640 cm.) Norton Simon Museum, Pasadena, Cal.
55. *MacDougal III*, 1972-1974. Cor-Ten steel. 48 x 120 x 48 in. (121.9 x 304.8 x 121.9 cm.)
56. *Lenox II*, 1975. Brass. 72 x 120 x 72 in. (182.9 x 304.8 x 182.9 cm.) Murray Financial Corporation, Dallas.
57. *Williams IIIa*, 1976. Steel. 76 x 112 x 70 in. (193.1 x 284.5 x 177.8 cm.)
58. *Ottumwa*, 1977-1978. 216 x 264 x 264 in. (548.6 x 670.5 x 670.5 cm.) Steel. City of Ottumwa, Iowa.
59. *Three Arches II*, 1962. Copper. 16 x 21 x 20 in. (40.6 x 53.3 x 50.8 cm.)
60. *Roanne*, 1978.

61. *Velay*, 1978. Brass. 35 x 19 x 16 in.
(88.9 x 48.2 x 40.6 cm.) Mr. and Mrs.
Robert Pergament, Kings Point, New York.
62. *Baldwin Hill*, 1979. Steel. 87 x 38 x 45 in.
(221 x 96.5 x 114.3 cm.)
63. *Homage to Piranesi X (Sens)*, 1978. Steel.
40 x 24 x 21 in. (101.6 x 60.9 x 53.3 cm.)
64. *Canaan II*, 1977-1978. Steel. 59 x 106 x 52 in.
(149.9 x 269.2 x 132 cm.)
65. *Bleeker*, 1978. Brass. 18½ x 24 x 19 in.
(46.9 x 60.9 x 48.3 cm.)
66. *Four Poles*, 1979. Steel. 61 x 54 x 38 in.
(154.9 x 137.2 x 96.5 cm.)
67. *Notch View*, 1978. Steel. 76 x 144 x 76 in.
(193.1 x 365.8 x 193.1 cm.) Diane and Steve
Jacobson, East Hampton, New York.
68. *Chesterwood*, 1979. Steel. 78 x 132 x 48 in.
(198.5 x 335.5 x 121.9 cm.)
69. *Wall Sculpture I*, 1979. Steel.
63¼ x 72 x 40 in. (160.6 x 182.9 x 101.6 cm.)
Richard Merrick, New York.
70. *Wall Sculpture III*, 1979. Steel.
63 x 80 x 38½ in. (160 x 203.2 x 97.79 cm.)
Private Collection, Houston.
71. Untitled, August 1949. Gouache on paper.
20¼ x 13⅛ in. (51.4 x 33.4 cm.)
72. *Rutgers #5*, 1959. Oil and magna on canvas.
90½ x 78½ in. (229.9 x 171.4 cm.)
73. Installation photograph. *Herbert Ferber:
Sculpture, Painting, Drawing 1945-1980.* The
Museum of Fine Arts, Houston.
74. Untitled, July 1971. Pen and ink, gouache,
and wash on paper. 9 x 19½ in.
(22.9 x 49.5 cm.)
75. Untitled, 1972. Gouache on paper.
9¹³⁄₁₆ x 15⅛ in. (24.9 x 38.4 cm.)
76. Installation photograph. *Herbert Ferber:
Sculpture, Painting, Drawing 1945-1980.* The
Museum of Fine Arts, Houston.
77. *Troilus*, 1980. Acrylic on canvas.
30 x 42 x 8 in. (76.2 x 106.7 x 20.3 cm.)
Collection Mr. Irwin Meyer, New York.
78. *Jug End*, 1981. Acrylic on canvas.
60 x 90 x 12 in. (152.4 x 228.6 x 30.5 cm.)
79. *When Yellow Leaves*, 1981. Acrylic on
canvas. 60 x 60 x 12 in.
(152.4 x 152.4 x 30.5 cm.)
80. Untitled, November 1979. Watercolor, ink
wash, and crayon on paper. 22¼ x 30 in.
(56.5 x 76.2 cm.)
81. Untitled, 2/1/48. Ink wash. 9½ x 12⅜ in.
(24.13 x 31.45 cm.)
82. Untitled, 6/50. Ink wash. 18⅝ x 24½ in.
(47.3 x 62.2 cm.)
83. Untitled, 1956. Ink wash. 24 x 19 in.
(60.9 x 48.3 cm.)
84. *Study for Three*, 1957. Ink wash.
15½ x 11¼ in. (39.4 x 28.6 cm.)
85. Untitled, 1960. Ink wash. 9½ x 12 in.
(24.1 x 30.5 cm.)
86. Untitled, 1961. Ink and wash. 13⅝ x 10⅛ in.
(34.6 x 25.7 cm.)

87. Untitled, 7/70. Watercolor. 12⅞ x 19 in.
(32.7 x 48.3 cm.)
88. Untitled, 1970. Ink wash and watercolor.
12¾ x 20 in. (32.4 x 50.8 cm.)
89. Untitled, 1971. Gouache and ink wash.
10⅝ x 16 in. (27 x 40.6 cm.)
90. Untitled, 1979. Ink wash and crayon.
10½ x 22½ in. (26.7 x 57.2 cm.)
91. Untitled, 9/79. Ink wash. 25⁵⁄₁₆ x 19½ in.
(64.3 x 49.5 cm.)

When no credit line is stated, the work is in
the collection of Herbert Ferber, Courtesy of M.
Knoedler & Co., Inc., New York.

Photographic Credits

Abrams Family Collection: 43

Albright-Knox Art Gallery: 26

Andre Emmerich Gallery, Inc.: 42

B'nai Israel Synogogue: 24

Rudolph Burckhardt: 15, 22, 25, 33

Congregation Beth Israel: 53

Louis H. Dreyer: 6

Edith Ferber: frontispiece, 1, 5, 12, 16, 50, 77, 78, 79

Herbert Ferber: 9, 11, 13, 14, 27, 31, 32, 36, 37, 38, 45,
46, 47, 48, 55, 57, 58, 59, 60, 62, 66, 68

Mr. and Mrs. Milton Gilbert: 51

Grand Rapids Art Gallery: 18

Bruce Gitlin: 44

Ruth Jacobi-Roth: 2, 3

Diane and Steve Jacobson: 67

John F. Kennedy Office Building: 41

M. Knoedler & Co., Inc.: 63, 64, 65, 70, 72

Richard Merrick: 69

Metropolitan Museum of Art: 4

A. Mewbourn: 8, 21, 71, 73, 74, 75, 76, 80, 81, 82, 83, 84,
85, 86, 87, 88, 89, 90, 91

Murray Financial Corporation: 56

The Museum of Modern Art: 17

National Gallery of Art: 35

Sharon and Neil Norry: 52

Norton Simon Museum: 54

Mr. and Mrs. Robert Pergament: 61

Mr. and Mrs. Robert Postal: 40

Eric Pollitzer: 23

Prudential Insurance Company of America: 30

Rutgers University Art Gallery: 7, 34

Storm King Art Center: 49

Whitney Museum of American Art: 19, 20, 28, 29